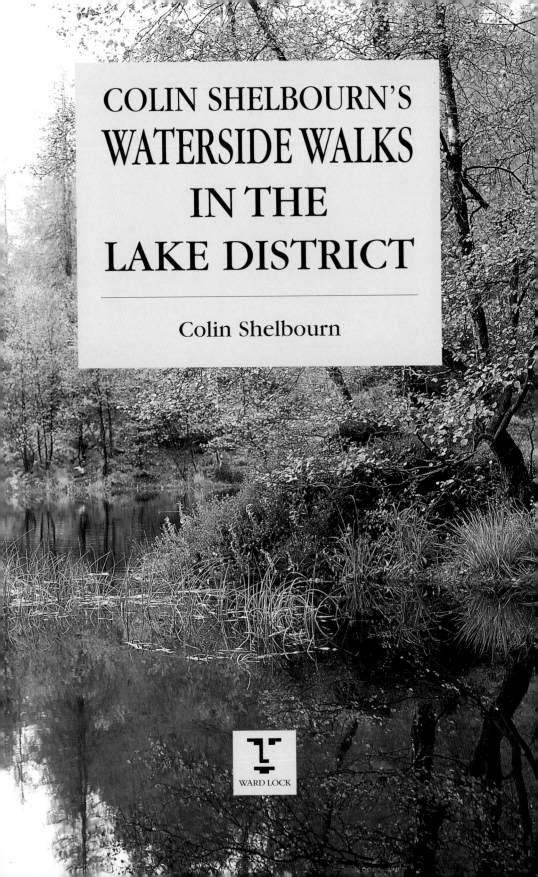

COLIN SHELBOURN'S
WATERSIDE WALKS
IN THE
LAKE DISTRICT

Colin Shelbourn

WARD LOCK

To P G

A WARD LOCK BOOK

First published in the UK 1998
by Ward Lock
Wellington House
125 Strand
LONDON
WC2R 0BB

A Cassell Imprint
Copyright Text © Colin Shelbourn 1998
Copyright Photographs © David Ward 1998
Copyright Maps © Colin Shelbourn 1998. Maps based on original
research compiled locally by the author. Map of walk locations based on
the Lake District Lap Map published by Cardtoons Publications Ltd.

Distributed in the United States
by Sterling Publishing Co., Inc.
387 Park Avenue South, New York, NY 10016-8810

A British Library Cataloguing in Publication Data block for this book may
be obtained from the British Library

ISBN 0 7063 7607 2

Designed by Chris Bell
Printed & bound in Slovenia by Printing House Delo Tiskarna d. d.
by arrangement with Korotan Ljubljana
Frontispiece: *Reflections of trees in the still waters of Low Dam*

CONTENTS

INTRODUCTION

There are far too many mountain summits in the Lake District. I'll rephrase that: if you are a keen walker, it is far too easy to be *lured* by the mountain summits. You dig out the map, think to yourself, 'Hmm, I've only climbed Scafell Pike 437 times but it's a while since I did it from Wasdale', and before you know it the sandwiches are made, the rucksack is packed and you are heading for the hills. Even worse, you might become a peak bagger, caught in the process of ticking off the summits like a hyperactive trainspotter.

If this description strikes a chord, it could be time to calm down and discover a secret. In addition to all the brown bits with the exciting contour lines, the Lake District also features significant amounts of blue. Within the boundary of the national park there are 16 lakes, over 400 tarns, and innumerable rivers, streams and waterfalls. They are all rich in wildlife, features and interest, each with a unique mood and atmosphere, and yet they are too often regarded as distractions to the serious business of climbing the high fells.

Waterside Walks in the Lake District seeks to redress this balance. By concentrating exclusively on routes which are along, around – and, in some cases, through – water, you will discover a whole new perspective on Lakeland.

The beauty of this approach is that the walks are so varied. This book covers everything from a simple 1km ($\frac{2}{3}$ mile) stroll to a 9km ($5\frac{1}{2}$ mile) hike into the mountains (I couldn't keep out of them entirely), and from exhilarating waterfalls to tranquil, isolated mountain tarns. It means there is something to suit a wide range of tastes and abilities, from families with small children to hardy types who fancy a day off from the high fells.

USING THE BOOK

The 25 walks are arranged by type and then in length order, with the shortest first. This broadly matches how much energy you will expend doing them. With the exception of the first, all the routes are circular, Ullswater and Derwent Water including a boat ride.

The final walk, across Morecambe Bay, is unusual for several reasons: it is outside the national park, it is off-shore and it doesn't get a route description. This is because it can only be done as an organized walk with the official guide. However, it is also a unique experience and had to be included. The description gives full details of when and how to join the walk.

Each route follows the direction which (in my opinion) gives the best views, defaulting, wherever possible, to follow the flow of rivers and becks. There is something curiously satisfying about this, but I haven't been too obsessive about it. I am not keen on books that break up the route descriptions with chunks of history or anecdotes, so these are distinguished from the main text with a tree symbol 🌳, and there is a note on the map so that you won't

The Howk cuts its way down through the limestone

5

miss any features of interest. At the end of each walk there are details of visitor attractions. The appendices give additional information which I hope will enhance your walking in the area. In Appendix 1 I've rounded up the remaining lakes and given a brief mention to a few extra favourite routes. Appendix 2 provides information about public transport for each of the 25 main walks, while Appendix 3 supplies useful addresses and additional tourist information about the area.

Bear in mind when doing these walks that many waterside habitats are fragile environments. Do not go scrambling into tarns and rivers if it means causing erosion or damaging the plant life. If you are tempted to swim, bear in mind that the water can be freezing cold; the lakes, in particular, remain cold throughout the year. Some of the lakes and tarns are plagued with blue-green algae in summer. This is unpleasant for all but actually dangerous for dogs and children, so if the water looks unclear, or you see warning notices, keep out.

On the subject of warnings, choose your footwear with care. Some of the walks become boggy in winter, but I have no idea how anyone stays upright in wellies on wet rock. For the longer routes, and the walks into the mountains, you will find proper walking boots much more comfortable. If you want information on boot hire – or on where you can hire baby buggies or backpacks – contact one of the tourist information centres listed in Appendix 3.

If you are unfamiliar with the Lake District, you will notice a few unusual phrases cropping up. 'Beck' is the local word for stream, 'force' is a waterfall and 'gill' (or 'ghyll') is a wooded valley, usually containing a stream. Many of these terms come from the Norse settlers, who probably also originated the Lakeland joke: How many lakes are there in the Lake District? One – Lake Bassenthwaite. All the others are 'waters' or 'meres'.

During the summer over which I researched this book, the weather varied from drought to torrential downpour. At one point there was so little water, I thought we might have to call it *Rubbleside Rambles*. Then the sky opened and several routes could not be researched because lakeshore paths were under water.

Throughout the walks, I was ably assisted by my chief researcher, Mannie, who also happens to be my dog. His contribution was invaluable; if any route involved keeping him on the lead for more than 50 per cent of the walk, it didn't make the book.

Finally, there are far too many Lakeland rivers and tarns for one book. If you get hooked, regard this as a starting point. Open one of the Ordnance Survey Outdoor Leisure Maps, select a speck of blue, find a right of way to it and go exploring. You will rarely be disappointed.

WALK LOCATIONS

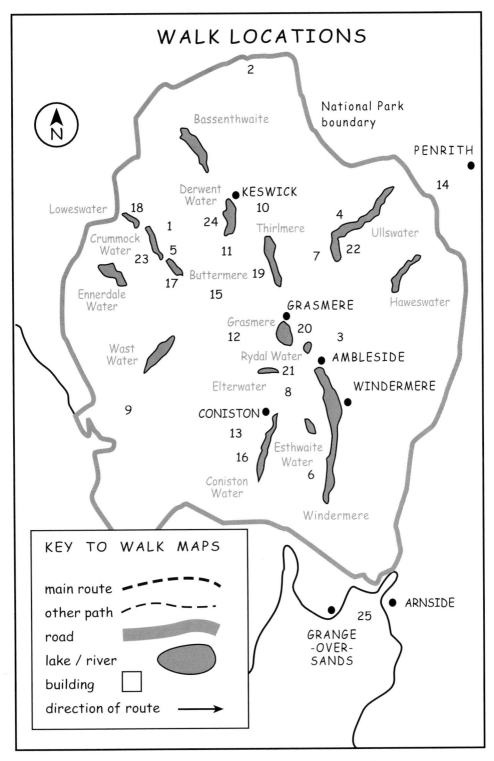

National Park boundary

Bassenthwaite

2

PENRITH

14

Loweswater

Derwent Water

KESWICK

10

18

1

24

Thirlmere

4

Ullswater

Crummock Water

5

11

7

22

23

Buttermere 19

17

15

Ennerdale Water

Haweswater

GRASMERE

Grasmere

20

12

3

Wast Water

Rydal Water

AMBLESIDE

21

WINDERMERE

Elterwater

8

9

CONISTON

13

Esthwaite Water

16

6

Coniston Water

Windermere

KEY TO WALK MAPS

main route	– – – –
other path	- - - -
road	▬▬▬
lake / river	⬭
building	☐
direction of route	⟶

ARNSIDE

25

GRANGE -OVER- SANDS

TARNS, RIVERS AND WATERFALLS

1 SPOUT FORCE

PARKING AND START/FINISH
There is very limited parking (three cars) in the quarry lay-by at Scawgill Bridge, 3.5km (2¼ miles) west of the Whinlatter Visitor Centre on the B5292 Braithwaite to Lorton road (GR 177257) The walk starts from this lay-by. Alternatively, use the Forest Enterprise car park, just off the B5292 at GR 182256 (about 0.5km/⅓ mile east of Scawgill Bridge)

DISTANCE
1km (⅔ mile)

TERRAIN
An extremely easy walk, with a short climb at the end

Previous pages:
The stone bridge
over the upper
falls of Aira Force

Spout Force is a waterfall for connoisseurs. It is not very famous or dramatic and is hidden in the hills, just off the Whinlatter Pass, making it easy to overlook as you speed past in the car. It is a leisurely stroll to reach it and there is an excellent viewpoint overlooking the waterfall.

F you have chosen the Forest Enterprise car park, you have a choice: either walk down the road to the Scawgill Bridge start, or follow the signs for Spout Force and then take the waymarked route across the fields and down the side of the gorge. A longer waymarked trail will eventually bring you back to the car park; I don't recommend retracing your route to return to the car park, as the pull up through the conifer forest is only for the extremely fit.

Starting from the Scawgill Bridge lay-by, look for the public footpath sign just before the bridge and go through the kissing gate. A path leads along the stone wall, just above the fast-flowing Aiken Beck. When you come to the next gate, take a moment to examine the amazing stone wall on your left. It consists of small slates, piled horizontally to climb the steep hillside – a very impressive example of the stone-waller's art.

Continue along the path, the river bordered by a larch wood on your left and a dark conifer wood on the right. The sides of the river valley rise very steeply. Look out for buzzards circling overhead (they have a cry not unlike a seagull). You will pass a wooden footbridge, where the path from the upper car park emerges from the trees. Continue following the river upstream and a set of steps will lead you into the larch wood. After a short climb up the side of the hill, the path leads you out to a fenced viewpoint and a surprise: a few metres in front of you, Spout Force gushes out of a deep cut in the hillside. This 7m (23ft) cascade is hidden in a sheltered cleft in the river valley. It is popular with climbers keen to practise their ice techniques when it freezes in winter.

To make the complete circuit, retrace your steps for a few metres. The path continues into the wood, climbing the hill on your right. This is the waymarked forest trail, but your route consists simply of following the outward path back to Scawgill Bridge.

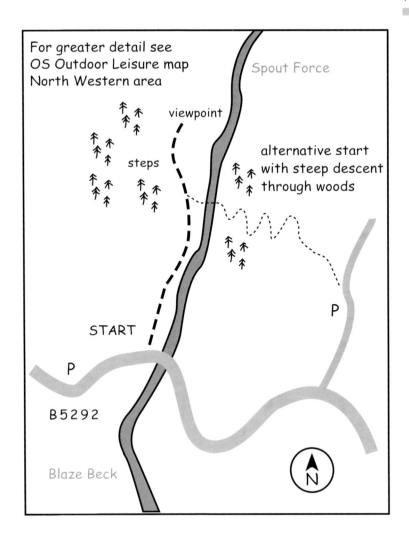

For greater detail see
OS Outdoor Leisure map
North Western area

Spout Force

viewpoint

steps

alternative start
with steep descent
through woods

START

P

P

B5292

Blaze Beck

N

VISITOR ATTRACTIONS

Whinlatter Visitor Centre
Whinlatter, Nr Keswick
Tel: 017687 78469
An excellent visitor centre 3.5km (2¼ miles) back along the road
towards Keswick. Features interactive exhibitions, displays and an
excellent café.

*The rushing
waters of Blaze
Beck, below
Spout Force*

2 THE HOWK, CALDBECK

PARKING AND START/FINISH
The walk starts from the National Park Authority car park just off the B5299, Caldbeck to Wigton road (GR 323399), signed 'Caldbeck Conservation Area'

DISTANCE
2km (1¼ miles)

TERRAIN
Very easy walking, but some sections are muddy in wet weather

This is an easy walk which takes you through one of north Cumbria's prettiest villages. The unusually named Howk is a waterfall which dashes through a picturesque limestone gorge, hidden in the woods on the western fringe of the village. Caldbeck has two recently restored mill buildings, with the opportunity to see a waterwheel in action.

WALK towards the far end of the car park past the level green areas, then turn up the little tarmac lane to the T-junction and the duck pond. Turn left and follow the lane to another T-junction, opposite Bridge End Stables. Walk straight across (look for the slate sign on the barn wall reading 'Footpath to the Howk'), through the stable yard and out again along the track on the far side. Whelpo Beck is across the field on your left. After about 30m (33yd), you will pass through a kissing gate and the wooded side of the gorge starts to rise up around you.

Glancing back to the village, you will notice a tall chimney stack among the houses. This is an old brew stack. The seventeenth-century building was probably once a fulling mill, used for processing sheep wool. During the nineteenth century it became a brewery, and in 1829 there were six pubs in the village.

Continuing on your way, you will pass a couple of small weirs and then come to the first of two mill buildings.

This building is a timber-drying store where wood was stacked for up to a year to get rid of moisture before it was made into bobbins. The bobbin mill was built in 1857 and at one time employed 60 men and boys. It had a waterwheel almost 13m (42ft) in diameter, the largest in the country. Alas, the wheel no longer exists, having been taken away and scrapped during World War II. The mill closed in 1920, but is now being restored by the Lake District National Park Authority.

Carry on past the mill, squeezing between the building and the wall of the ravine. You are now walking upstream, past a series of small cascades, and after about 50m (54yd) you will come to a flight of stone steps. Climb the first dozen or so and suddenly you will have a view of the Howk.

14

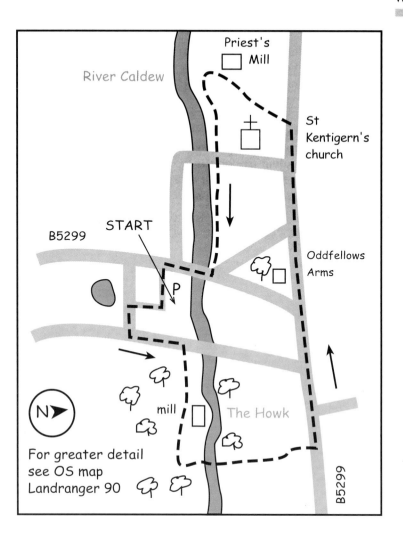

The waterfall cuts through the limestone just below you, forming a bowl. It is sheltered by the rock and the surrounding trees, forming a very pretty view, especially in spring. Continue up the steps and turn left, following the handrail down to a wooden footbridge. The path splits at this point. Straight ahead the path continues to another, smaller waterfall (which is worth a diversion) and then heads out across the fields to Whelpo. Your route goes left, over the footbridge, and provides another opportunity to view the Howk.

Once over the bridge and up another flight of steps, leave the woods via a kissing gate and head straight across the field to another kissing gate (look for the farm building and four tall pines ahead of you: the gate is just to the right). Crossing the field is very tranquil after the noise and drama of the Howk, and you will have a

15

good view to High Pike and the Caldbeck Fells in the distance. (But not, unfortunately, to the second best-named fell, Great Cockup, which lies just behind the Caldbeck hills. For the best-named fell, see Walk 23: Crummock Water & Mosedale Beck.)

When you leave the field you are on the B5299, so put dogs on leads. It is not a busy road, but there is always the chance of meeting a young farmer on a souped-up tractor. Turn left and follow the road back into the village. Go past the junction of roads, with the map shop and walnut tree on the triangle in the middle, and continue through the village. As you cross another beck, look out for the clogmaker's shop on the right.

♪ Caldbeck village gets its name from the Norse description of the stream, kaldr beck – cold stream. It developed originally as a rural settlement, until lead, copper and coal were discovered in the surrounding fells. During the eighteenth century the village became a centre for rural industry, with mills springing up along the river to spin wool, grind corn, and make paper and bobbins.

Priest's Mill, built at the beginning of the eighteenth century, was originally used for grinding corn

After about 10 minutes you will pass St Kentigern's church on your left. Cross over and walk down the lane past the church, signed 'Priest's Mill'.

🔔 *Priest's Mill was built in 1702 by the rector of St Kentigern's. It was originally a corn mill, power coming from a waterwheel 4m (13ft) in diameter. The mill was sold by the church in 1901 and continued working as first a corn mill and then a saw mill. It was still working as a joiner's workshop until 1967, when it fell into disuse. Restoration work began in 1985.*

The earliest part of St Kentigern's church is a Norman archway, dating back to 1112. An earlier wooden church probably once stood on this spot. The present building is mostly late medieval, although a great deal of restoration was carried out in 1880. St Kentigern (sometimes known as St Mungo) was the sixth-century Bishop of Glasgow. Just behind the church is a road known as Friar Row; the name comes from a hospice that was maintained here in medieval times by the Prior of Carlisle.

St Kentigern's most famous resident is John Peel, the huntsman and subject of the song 'D'ye ken John Peel?' He died in 1854 and his grave is in the churchyard, on the left.

The lane leads you to Priest's Mill car park. At the bottom, turn left and follow the churchyard wall to a small bridge over Cald Beck. Just past the bridge, look out for St Kentigern's Well, a small trough on the riverbank. Then, without crossing the bridge, continue along the narrow path, past the rectory, to the road. Turn right, cross over two bridges, and you arrive back at the entrance to the car park.

VISITOR ATTRACTIONS

Priest's Mill
Caldbeck, Nr Penrith
Tel: 016974 78369
A very carefully converted former water mill, now the home of an excellent café, bookshop, jewellery craft shop and a number of other attractions. Don't miss the mill museum at the back, where for a nominal fee you can set the mill wheel in operation.

3 STOCKGHYLL FORCE

PARKING AND START/FINISH
There are several good car parks in Ambleside but the best is the South Lakeland District Council car park on Rydal Road (the A591 Ambleside to Grasmere road), with its entrance opposite Charlotte Mason College. The walk starts from this car park

DISTANCE
2km (1¼ miles)

TERRAIN
The path is good in dry weather but can be muddy in winter. Steep in places, with a stretch of potentially slippery rock to negotiate on the way down

Harriet Martineau, the diarist and close friend of Wordsworth, said of Stockghyll Force: 'It is the fashion to speak lightly of this waterfall – it being within half a mile of the inn, and so easily reached; but it is, in our opinion, a very remarkable fall (from the symmetry of its parts) and one of the most graceful that can be seen.' Once you have completed this walk, you will agree that Stockghyll is a hidden treasure – a superb waterfall within 15 minutes' walk of the centre of Ambleside, ideal for families with young children or anyone who wants to escape the shops and traffic for an hour.

BEFORE embarking on the walk, you should note that there is now a waymarked route to the waterfall, resulting in a number of intrusive red arrows appearing in Stock Ghyll park. Do not be distracted by these: follow the route described throughout.

Leave the car park via the footbridge and turn right along the pavement. The peculiar small stone house on your right is known as the Bridge House and is built over Stock Beck. The interesting buildings behind are an innovative glass workshop, gallery and restaurant run by Adrian Sankey.

Built between 1650 and 1700, the Bridge House has a long and varied history, and at various times has been a weaver's shop, a cobbler's, an antique shop and a tea room. Incredibly, it was also once a family home and six children were raised here. They must have been very small and well behaved: the main room measures less than 4×2m (13×6½ft). There is an old legend that it was constructed by a canny Scotsman to avoid land tax, but in fact it was originally the apple store belonging to Ambleside Hall, which used to stand on the corner of North Road and Smithy Row, when this part of the town was an orchard. The Bridge House is now a National Trust shop and information centre.

Just over the road bridge, cross the road to Bridge Street, the small alley (or 'ginnel') directly opposite Dodd's Restaurant which is signed 'Footpath to North Road, Old Bark Mill'. Once known by the more picturesque name of Rattle Gill, this cobbled alley leads you between some of the oldest houses in Ambleside. You will pass under the first storey of one of the houses and then emerge by the

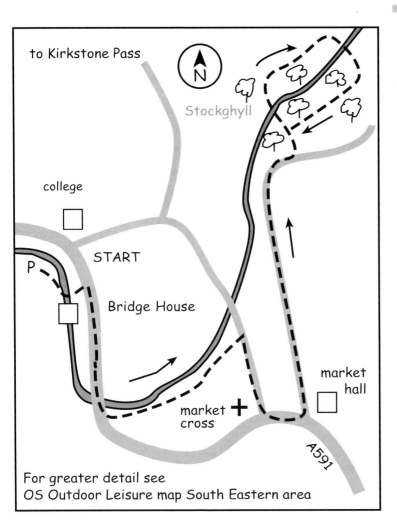

to Kirkstone Pass

N

Stockghyll

college

START

P

Bridge House

market
hall

market
cross

A591

For greater detail see
OS Outdoor Leisure map South Eastern area

river, alongside the old waterwheel: Stock Ghyll once powered three woollen mills in addition to corn, linen, paper and saw mills.

Turn right at the road and into the middle of Ambleside. Note the market cross on your right as you come to the main road, then turn left past the Salutation Hotel and make your way up another alley between Barclays Bank and Bertram's Restaurant, which is in the old Market Hall.

Ambleside received its market charter in 1650 and it is from that date that the present town developed. Prior to that, the medieval village had grown along North Road, on the packhorse route up Kirkstone Pass.

This brings you to a lane called Cheapside. Turn left (signed 'To the waterfalls') and continue uphill. This is a quiet lane with little traffic, which runs alongside Stock Beck. The building on the far bank was once a mill, briefly became a holiday complex, and now consists largely of holiday homes. After about five minutes' walking, just past the entrance to Stock Ghyll Croft turn left off the road and into Stock Ghyll Park.

The path takes you through a wood and alongside the river. Look out for the old dam, just as you pass the first of the park benches. Once past another bench and a set of wooden steps, the path forks. Go left, making your way down steps to a wooden footbridge. This acts as a collecting point for branches washed down the river at times of high rainfall. As you cross, you can see the tree-lined river gorge opening up ahead of you. The path now climbs steeply above the level of the river. The sides of the gorge are covered with mosses, plants and a sprinkling of trees. If you keep close to the metal fence, it will lead you to a good view of Stockghyll Force and its pools.

Retrace your steps to the path and continue up to the wooden bridge at the top of the waterfall. Once over, continue right, following the metal fence downhill. Take care as you go past the wooden picnic table and cross a rock outcrop, which gets very slippery when wet. Just past the next bench there is another picnic table and the path forks. The path down is to the right, but if you go left you can take a look at the wonderful Victorian turnstile at the upper entrance to the park.

The wooden foot-bridge spanning Stockghyll Force

♪ *The 18m (60ft) drop of Stockgbyll Force was a popular visitor attraction in Victorian times. They built the bridges and installed the iron railings and the gate at the top. Visitors were charged 3d (about 1p) to see the waterfall.*

The helpfully handrailed path back down through Stock Ghyll park to Ambleside

Return to the path and continue downhill. Once again, look out for the viewpoints thoughtfully provided by the Victorians. The first of these occurs just past a set of concrete steps: double around the tree and there is an excellent view of the waterfall. The second one is a few hundred metres (yards) further on – the metal fence stops in the tree trunk.

Continuing downhill, you will pass a small house on the left and then join the outward path. Retrace your route into Ambleside, where you can make use of one of the many cafés in the town.

VISITOR ATTRACTIONS

The Bridge House is a National Trust information centre and is open throughout the year.

Adrian Sankey's Glass House
Rydal Road, Ambleside
Tel: 015394 37346
Just behind the Bridge House is an imaginative development which features a glass workshop where you can purchase glassware, hand blown on site, plus an attractive restaurant.

4 AIRA FORCE

PARKING AND START/FINISH

The walk starts from the National Trust pay-and-display car park at the junction of the A592 Glenridding to Pooley Bridge road and the A5091 to Dockray. There is also a free car park less than a mile along the A5091. From this car park, walk across the field to join the walk from the upper bridge

DISTANCE

2km (1¼ miles)

TERRAIN

Very easy walking to Aira Force, making it ideal for families and junior walkers. A few tree roots and rocks to scramble over to reach the upper bridge

Aira Force is Lakeland's best-known waterfall and is heavily promoted as such by the National Trust, which owns the surrounding land. This means that in summer you could be queuing up to the use the car park, and the path to the falls will be engulfed by coach parties. It is worth the effort to go early in the day or late in the afternoon, for when you can get it to yourself the waterfall is magical.

A T the back of the National Trust car park there is a slate canopy and an information point. Go through the archway alongside this and follow the path through the shady pine woods. Once through the second gate, you will be able to see the river on your right. Go through a wooden gate and between two yew trees, and you will come to a footbridge. Once across, the path splits two ways, beside another large yew tree. This is a pleasant, open area and a strong indicator of the days when it was all part of Gowbarrow Park.

🔊 *It was along this part of the shores of Ullswater that William Wordsworth spotted a host of golden daffodils. Although he later claimed to be wandering lonely as a cloud, he and his sister Dorothy were walking together to visit their friend Thomas Clarkson, the anti-slave trade campaigner who lived at Eusemere (near Pooley Bridge). Dorothy's diary for 15 April 1802 reads:*

> *I never saw daffodils so beautiful, they grew among the mossy stones about and about them, some resting their heads upon these stones as a pillow for weariness and the rest tossed and reeled and danced and seemed as if they verily laughed with the wind that blew upon them over the lake, they looked so gay ever glancing ever changing.*

These notes later became the inspiration for William's famous poem.

Walk straight ahead and follow the wooden fence to the gap and the steps down to the footbridge over Aira Beck. Once you've crossed, disregard the path which goes left along the bank and walk up the steps to climb above the river. The path splits again about 40m (43yd) further on, just below a massive Scots pine.

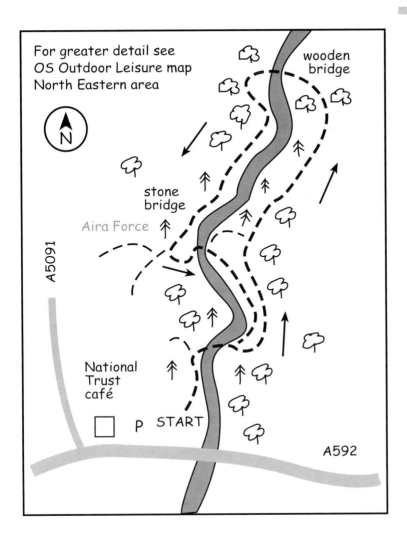

For greater detail see
OS Outdoor Leisure map
North Eastern area

N

stone
bridge

Aira Force

A5091

National
Trust
café

p START

wooden
bridge

A592

Although this is taking you away from the river, go right; the path
then climbs to give you a view of Ullswater and Place Fell. Keep
inside the fence (don't cross the stile where the path forks), and
just past a park bench the path forks again. Go left again, downhill
towards the sound of the river in the wooded ravine ahead.

You will pass a rock outcrop and come to the stone bridge over
the upper falls. This is a good viewpoint, but don't cross it for now.
Instead, go right, following the river upstream and ignoring the
steps off to the right, about 20m (22yd) past the bridge. This is a
lovely, wooded walk, climbing past a series of small cascades, with
plenty of places to dabble hot paws. The path is rougher and narrower but keeps to the river throughout. There is a bit of scrambling over rocks and tree roots. It comes to an apparent stop on a
ledge, overlooking a gorge and a long cascade. The rock has been

23

A view through trees of Aira Beck, above Aira Force

cut away by the water and the trees overhang the ravine to create a very cool, picturesque spot. As an added bonus, few of the crowds who come to see Aira Force bother to explore this far, so you may be lucky and get it to yourself.

Just before the ledge there is a path to the right. Walk up it and bear left, to continue upstream. After 10m (11yd) turn left and you will see a wooden bridge ahead. After another 20m (22yd) the path zigzags right to join another track. Turn left and shortly afterwards left again. You are now climbing above the ravine but heading upstream once more. After another 50m (54yd) the path forks again. Go left and walk down to the wooden bridge. It stands over a very narrow gully which is dark and mossy. Notice the rowan tree, emerging from the side of the gully at a right angle.

Once over the bridge, walk straight on, following a wire fence for about 25m (27yd) before heading downhill again. Don't be tempted by the erosion path lower down, close to the riverbank; the upper path is rocky in places. You will eventually drop to the level of the river and back to the upper bridge. Don't cross but go right, up a few steps, and then the path descends once more. It takes you into a clearing, to a bench seat and a view of Helvellyn.

The path splits here. Take the left fork and walk down 103 steps to the classic view of Aira Force. Make use of the handrail, as the slate steps can get very slippery. As you descend carefully, you will feel the temperature drop and the air freshen. The steps bring you down to the lower bridge, from where you can look straight up the waterfall to the upper bridge. After a heavy thaw you will need to wear waterproofs to stand here for any length of time.

🔊 *Aira Force is a spectacular sight. A 21m (70ft) cascade cuts through the rocks and crashes into a deep pool. Ten years ago, when writing about this fall I commented that the sound of the water is drowned by the click of shutters; today, I should add the whirr of motor drives and the flash of automatic cameras. It has been a popular spot for centuries. In 1835 Wordsworth described it in his* Guide to the English Lakes *as 'a powerful brook which dashes among rocks through a deep glen, hung on every side with a rich and happy intermixture of native wood.'*

Continue over the bridge and follow the path downhill. Ignore the steps coming in from the left after about 30m (35yd) - this way round, the walk is designed to minimize step climbing!. The path winds its way along the side of the wooded ravine, while tall pines tower above, giving the feel of a vaulted cathedral roof. The path then drops down towards the level of the river and arrives back at the first wooden bridge. Cross back over the bridge and retrace your steps to the start of the walk.

VISITOR ATTRACTIONS
See Walk 22: Ullswater.

5 MILL BECK, BUTTERMERE

PARKING AND START/FINISH
The walk starts from the National Trust pay-and-display car park on the B5289, just outside Buttermere village, on the Crummock Water side. Parking is much easier here than in the car park in the village centre

DISTANCE
2.75km (1¾ miles), including the 0.5km (⅓ mile) digression to Crummock Water shore

TERRAIN
An easy stroll down to the river, followed by a not-too-strenuous climb to the waterfall. Good grip is recommended in the wet, as the waterfall section can become muddy and slippery

Driven by the desire to circle the lake, most visitors to Buttermere village overlook this little walk. They are missing out. This is a short stroll which follows Mill Beck to Crummock Water and then heads upstream into a dark gorge, to a fascinating series of cascades above Buttermere village.

LEAVE the car park via the kissing gate on the north side and join the main path from the road, turning left and heading into Long How wood. The path leads down through the trees to Mill Beck, a delightful river which flows from below Newlands Hause to Crummock Water.

The way runs right along the riverbank, below an outcrop of rock. The path has been worked extensively by the National Trust so, as you might expect, it is level and dead easy to follow. You will get glimpses across the fields to Red Pike and Sour Milk Gill. The other two becks, cascading down the fell at the head of Crummock, are the imaginatively named Far and Near Ruddy Beck. I'll let you guess which is which.

As you reach the footbridge, there is a tantalizing glimpse of Crummock Water ahead. Cross the bridge and go over the stile into the field. The route goes left (signed 'Buttermere Village & Scale Bridge & Force') but you should take a diversion right and follow the path along the river and into Nether How wood. This brings you to a pebbly beach at the southern end of Crummock and provides a magnificent view along the lake to Mellbreak and Grasmoor. If you haven't already done it, the Crummock Water walk follows the far western shore below Mellbreak and climbs up behind the mountain on the left, over the saddle between Mellbreak and Gale Fell.

Make your way back to the river and stile and head towards Buttermere village. You will be walking alongside the river beneath trees, and gradually Fleetwith Pike and Haystacks will come into view at the far end of Buttermere. The path bears left through a gap in the fence and runs between the river and the field boundary, spurning the footbridge to Syke Farm. It then brings you into

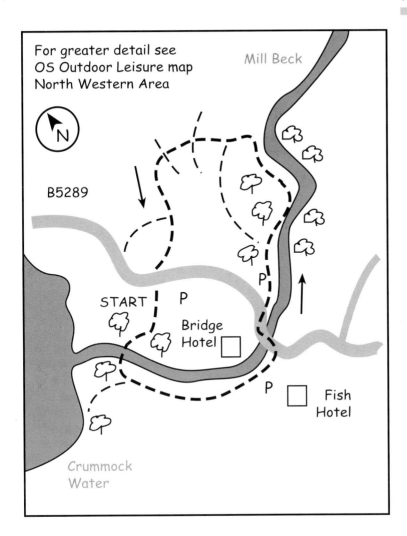

For greater detail see
OS Outdoor Leisure map
North Western Area

Mill Beck

B5289

START

Bridge
Hotel

P

P

Fish
Hotel

Crummock
Water

the National Park Authority car park. Walk up through the car park, past the toilet block and café, averting your eyes from the picturesque holiday apartments behind the Bridge Hotel. You will come out on the road beside the hotel: turn left, then immediately over the road bridge turn right and enter Ghyll Wood to rejoin Mill Beck (so named because it fed the corn mill which once stood on the site now occupied by the Bridge Hotel).

A clear path now takes you through a delightful woodland, climbing alongside the river gorge. At the confluence of the two rivers there is a small waterfall. Look out for the ferns covering the rocks and thriving in the dark, damp atmosphere. About 100m (110yd) further uphill the path forks. The left-hand option climbs gradually to the top of the wood, but if you are feeling fit go right, which has the best views. This path drops down to the riverbank

Right: *Sunlight through trees in Long How wood, at the start of the walk*

Opposite: *Mill Beck cascades down through its wooded, fern-clad gorge*

and winds along the side of the gorge, giving you the opportunity to enjoy the vigorous torrent as it plunges between the rocks. Look out for the weird and wacky oak tree growing over the river and covered in ferns and moss.

At the footbridge, turn left for a steep, thigh-burning pull to the top of the wood. The easier path now comes in from the left. There's an unusual ladder stile, complete with integral gate, which takes you out of the trees and on to open fellside. You now have a choice. Turning left takes you down alongside the wall and fence line and back to the road, opposite the car park where you started. It is the easier of the two routes and you get good views of Buttermere, but they are not the best. For those, you should go straight up through the bracken, keeping to the distinct path, and straight over at the next two crossroads of paths. From the second crossing you will start to descend. Divert to stand on top of the outcrop on your left and you will gain a brilliant view of Buttermere.

Rejoining the path, keep going down, heading towards a large, rocky knoll on your right. Where the path splits, go right, winding below the crag and alongside a bog. As you approach the fence line, a small beck runs alongside the path. The latter swings left around the crag and runs downhill beside the field boundary, to emerge on the road opposite the main entrance to Long How wood. Go through the gate and turn left, back to the car park and starting point.

VISITOR ATTRACTIONS

See Walk 10: River Greta.

6 FINSTHWAITE TARN

PARKING AND START/FINISH
If visiting the Stott Park Bobbin Mill, park at their car park and use the off-road footpath to High Dam. Or, use the small free car park below High Dam, from which the walk starts. This is on the Lakeside to Finsthwaite road, signed 'Finsthwaite, Rusland and Satterthwaite'. Coming from Lakeside, the turning is the first on the right, past the village sign for Finsthwaite

DISTANCE
2.75km (¾ miles), excluding the walk to Stott Park Bobbin Mill

TERRAIN
A climb to High Dam, then a mostly level walk around the tarn. Can be muddy in places

This is a two-part walk: after you have explored the reservoir, there is the opportunity to visit the bobbin mill it was built to power. In recent years, the area around the tarn has been developed and improved by the National Park Authority and is now a serious rival to the National Trust's Tarn Hows. In my opinion, Finsthwaite is the better of the two – quieter, more mysterious and far more of an adventure to discover.

THE car park for High Dam is tucked away in the trees at the top of a narrow tarmac lane. There is no passing traffic, so the walk begins immediately you've got your boots on. Head uphill into the woods, away from the lane. You are accompanied by a strong beck which comes crashing over the rocks on your left. Although narrow, the beck has several short cascades which are worth looking out for.

The track leads to a farm gate and kissing gate. On the other side, the route forks. The track goes right, but you should follow the path straight ahead. After about 100m (110yd), ignore the footbridge over the beck and continue up the stony path. You are now walking through heavily coppiced woodland of birch and oak.

Coppicing is the practice of cutting back birch, oak and ash saplings to provide the raw material for charcoal burning (and other species for a variety of uses). The area around Rusland and Backbarrow supported a number of mills and furnaces and the surrounding woods are heavily coppiced. Birch was also used for making the bobbins and reels which supplied the thriving nineteenth-century Lancashire cotton industry. A large mill could make use of around a million bobbins a week.

Demonstrations of charcoal burning can sometimes be seen at Brantwood, John Ruskin's home at Coniston. Contact Coniston tourist information centre for details (see Appendix 3).

Continue climbing through the trees, accompanied by the constant hiss and roar of the beck. At the stone wall, go through a second kissing gate and keep straight on, ignoring the path off to the right. After another 200m (220yd) or so you will enter a band of fir trees and arrive at the first dam. It stands at the foot of a

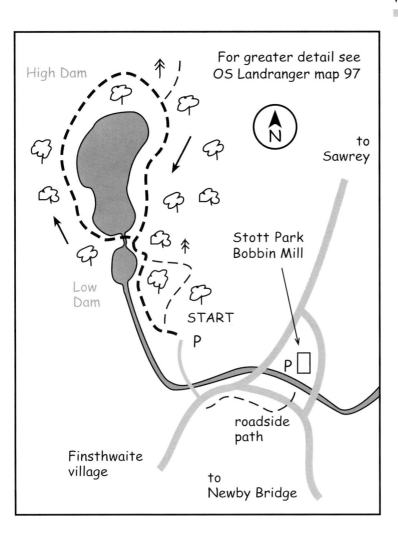

High Dam

For greater detail see
OS Landranger map 97

N

to
Sawrey

Stott Park
Bobbin Mill

Low
Dam

START

P

P

roadside
path

Finsthwaite
village

to
Newby Bridge

small, pretty reservoir, surrounded by fir trees. This is Low Dam and there is a path across it and around the other side. However, as it can be very muddy and difficult to follow, resist the temptation and continue uphill. After crossing two footbridges, you will come to High Dam. Both dams were developed in 1835 from the original Finsthwaite Tarn, to provide power for the waterwheel at Stott Park Mill.

High Dam is smaller than Tarn Hows but, in my opinion, more interesting. It is much less cultivated and, surrounded by larch woods, it has a dark, mysterious air – it is easy to feel very isolated here. At the wall, turn left and cross the dam. Look out for the valve for the outflow pipe, in the water on your right. This was installed when a turbine was used to power the bobbin mill at Stott Park, replacing an earlier waterwheel.

*Finsthwaite Tarn
seen from the
southern shore*

The wall is about 100m (110yd) long. At the end, you plunge into the trees of a dense larch wood. These provide a thick overhead canopy but are not too closely planted, allowing plenty of room for other vegetation to thrive. The path is easy to follow. The simple rule is that where it branches off, you should stick to the shore. The path winds along the shore past the island and then crosses a beck and goes through a stone wall. The path forks, the left-hand option signed to Rusland. Go straight, along the clearer path, and after 50m (54yd) or so you begin to climb away from the tarn and up the side of Great Green Hows. On reaching a wire fence, bear right along it, parallel to the low ridge on your left. After five minutes' steady walking, you will glimpse the tarn again. Arriving at a wooden seat, you will have a lovely view across the tarn to Gummer's How in the distance.

The path drops downhill and over another beck. After another 50m (54yd) you reach the wide, open marsh at the head of the tarn. The path here is very clear. At one time you walked across via a series of wooden board walks, but latterly the National Park has built a neat cinder path, underlaid with plastic matting. It keeps the path clear of mud and gives it a curiously spongy feel as you march across past gorse and heather, and then you are back into the woods. This is mixed woodland for a short way and then you encounter larch again. Ignore the path off to the right, which heads to the stone wall, and continuing winding round to the tarn, which comes back into view after 100m (110yd) or so.

The final part of the walk is a delightful stroll along the bank, winding through mixed woodland with constant views over the water. Look out for the bench by the water – a brilliant spot for a picnic. Eventually the path brings you back to the dam wall and you can retrace your steps to the car. Note that below the top kissing gate there is a broad track off to the left – this will take you down to the lower gate, while avoiding the steeper parts of the path.

Once back at your car, it is worth making the short walk to Stott Park Bobbin Mill, which was, after all, the whole purpose for the tarn being developed. Walk down the lane to the main road and turn left. After about 50m (54yd) there is a path on the far side of the road, signed 'Permitted Footpath to Stott Park Bobbin Mill'. Follow this path and it will bring you out opposite the car park entrance to the mill.

🏭 *Stott Park Mill was built in 1835 by John Harrison, a gentleman farmer, originally to supply bobbin reels to the cotton industry. It was one of the Lake District's most important mills and continued producing bobbins until it closed in 1971. English Heritage bought the site and reopened it as a museum in 1983. The two original curators used to work in the industry (although not at Stott Park) and were able to give wonderful guided tours and demonstrations. The mill is located as close as possible to its raw materials, in this case water power from Finsthwaite Tarn and birch from the local woodland.*

VISITOR ATTRACTIONS

Stott Park Bobbin Mill
Finsthwaite, Newby Bridge
Tel: 0191 2611585
See route description for details.

Lakeside and Haverthwaite Railway
Newby Bridge
Tel: 015395 31594
This restored section of the Lakeside to Ulverston line is run by enthusiasts, with steam trains connecting Haverthwaite to the boat services at Lakeside.

Windermere Iron Steamboat Co.
Lakeside, Newby Bridge
Tel: 015395 31188
Large cruisers which run throughout the summer, including special evening cruises.

Bowness Bay Boating Company
Bowness-on-Windermere
Tel: 015394 43468
Smaller launches running throughout the year, linking Ambleside, Brockhole, Bowness and Lakeside.

Lakeside Aquatarium
Lakeside, Newby Bridge
Tel: 015395 30153
Tells the story of a Lakeland mountain stream, including fascinating fish, insect and plant life. It is open all year and is highly recommended.

7 LANTY'S TARN

PARKING AND START/FINISH
The walk starts from the National Park Authority pay-and-display car park in the village centre (follow signs for the tourist information centre) (GR 385169)

DISTANCE
3.5km (2¼ miles)

TERRAIN
A steep climb to the tarn up an excellent footpath, then an easy descent along Miresbeck

Lanty's Tarn is a lovely little reservoir hidden in the hills above Glenridding. It is surrounded by trees and easily missed in the mad rush to get to the top of Helvellyn. While the vigorous, hardy types toil up the mountain to tick off another summit, you can do this walk and enjoy some unusual views of Ullswater, with a gentle meander back alongside Miresbeck and Glenridding Beck.

THE car park has one or two interesting points. Look around and you'll spot a footpath sign pointing to the far corner which bears the single, laconic word 'Helvellyn'.

This is a regular starting point for the climb of one of the big four Lakeland mountains. At 950m (3088ft) high, it is probably the most rewarding of the major peaks and it attracts walkers like a magnet. Unfortunately, not all of them realize what they are letting themselves in for: on one memorable occasion in late autumn, I encountered a gentleman on Striding Edge wearing jeans and carrying a collapsible umbrella in his rucksack. On that particular day the peak was covered in thick mist, and a National Park ranger was stationed on the summit to advise people how to get back down.

Scots pines on Keldas, with Ullswater beyond

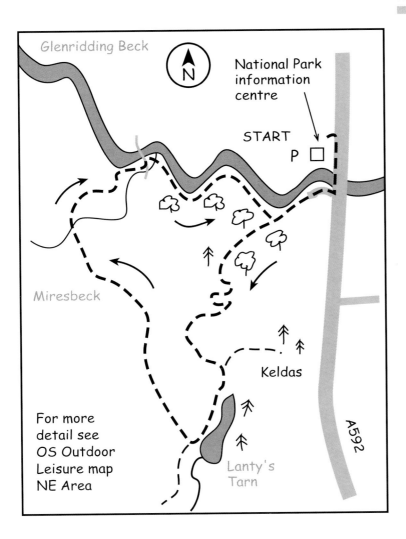

Visit the National Park Authority information centre in the car park, and you will find a fascinating relief model of the Helvellyn range.

Walking back to the entrance, you will pass the National Park Authority tourist information centre, which has a mining cart on display outside. There is an excellent, larger display about Greenside Mine inside.

♤ *Greenside Mine was established in the seventeenth century to mine lead and silver. In fact, the history of mining in this area probably goes back to Roman times. The mine was very productive throughout the eighteenth and nineteenth centuries: in 1875 it produced lead and silver worth over £1 million, thus proving to be one of the most profitable in England. Ore was carried by packhorse*

37

*to Keswick or Alston Moor and then, with the coming of the railways,
to Newcastle. The mine pioneered the use of electric locomotives
and winders to work the shafts. Mining ended in 1962, although
local enthusiasts still explore the levels and set off occasional test
explosions.*

Leave the car park via the main entrance, turn right to cross the
road bridge and then turn right again immediately before
Sharman's grocery store (signed 'Public Bridleway: Mires Beck,
Helvellyn'). How many other local grocers do you know who hire
out mountain boots? Turning up the narrow lane alongside
Glenridding Beck, you will pass Catsycam outdoor store, a couple
of houses and Glenridding public hall. Continue past the kennels
and along the track through Eagle Farm. About 200m (220yd) past
the barns, the track forks. You will then be coming back along the
right-hand track (unless you get hopelessly lost), so take the left
fork (signed 'Lanty's Tarn, Helvellyn'). You now begin to get a good
view right into Greenside and along the valley to the old mine
workings.

Walk on past The Croft, an attractive Lakeland stone terrace,
and the path then forks. You can go either way, but if you go left –
through the narrow gate and past the garden – you will cross a
footbridge and come out alongside a small waterfall in the trees.
Go right – passing the alternative gate – and follow the path up the
hillside. The going is a bit rough here, but you will quickly reach
the maintained section.

As you climb the field, you will have a good view back across
the valley to Glenridding Dodd and Sheffield Pike. Walk up alongside a wire fence and, as the path goes left around it, stop at the
wooden bench seat and take in the view of Ullswater – a small hint
of what is to come.

Climb on up to a kissing gate and, once through, the path leads
you to the right across open fellside (signed 'Lanty's Tarn, Grisedale
& Striding Edge'). You now have a very good view into the valley
below. Turn around slightly and you can take in Ullswater and
Place Fell. The path leads to a stone wall and forks again. Go left,
continuing uphill and enjoying better and better views. At the top
of the field you get a real panorama: Ullswater and Place Fell,
around to Gowbarrow Park and Ulph's Tower, and farther left to
Glenridding Dodd and Sheffield Pike. The path drops to a kissing
gate in a stone wall, but before going through it is worth a 15-
minute diversion to the left to climb Keldas, the pine-covered
knoll. From here you have a 360-degree view of the surrounding
fells. You can look down into Grisedale, left to Place Fell and on to
Ullswater, appreciating the distinct bend in the shape of the lake.
Walk back to the kissing gate, go through and you will arrive at
Lanty's Tarn.

♤ *Lanty's Tarn was once entirely natural. Its name is a contraction of Lancelot's Tarn, after Lancelot Dobson, the last man to own the tarn before it became a reservoir. He sold it in the 1820s to the Marshall family, the owners of Patterdale Hall (which is now the Patterdale Youth Hostel). They dammed the outflow and used the tarn for fishing in summer and for making ice in winter. The tarn is around 2m (6½ feet) deep.*

This is a lovely spot. The tarn is flanked by conifer plantations and there are birch trees along the edge of the water. It is very quiet here, with no sound of rushing water and just the occasional bleat of a solitary sheep. Walk to the end of the tarn (ignoring the path which goes right, at the end of the fence) and you come to the concrete dam wall. A clear track leads down from this into Grisedale, but look right and level with the wall you will spot a narrower path, heading up the side of the small hill on your right. Take this path and you will climb away from the tarn, towards Dollywagon Pike and Helvellyn. Look left and you can see into the valley, up to St Sunday Crag and, a little farther left, glimpse the straight ridge of High Street between the peaks in the distance.

The path takes you around the little grassy knoll on to open fell, heading towards a group of conifers. You can go straight on to the conifers or bear right across the slightly boggy field. Either way, you are heading towards the stone wall and gate you can see on the skyline to your right. At the gate there is another terrific view: High Street and Place Fell on your right, Ullswater and then the flat top of Glenridding Dodd, with Sheffield Pike and Raise to the left.

Go through the gate, heading towards Swart Beck – the white streak on the fell to the left of Sheffield Pike. Crossing a couple of minor becks, you then head around the fellside along an easy path which follows the contour of the hill. Make your way around the end of the fell and over two larger becks, and you will then begin dropping towards a stone wall and a deciduous wood. The crag rising in front of you is the Nab, part of Birkhouse Moor. Once at the wall, keep going straight and you will begin to hear the rush of water. When you reach the end of the wall you have arrived at Miresbeck. Cross the beck and turn right, over another beck and heading downhill, in the direction of Glenridding and Ullswater. You then drop down to a farm gate and ladder stile and, once through, will find yourself on a rough vehicle track, heading downhill through the field.

The track drops down to an isolated cottage. Turn left, following the track to another set of gates and a T-junction. The left turn is signed 'Greenside Mines' but you go right, continuing down the track to cross the river and join a tarmac lane. Turn left along the lane and walk to a crossroads. On your left is a very neat caravan park. Go right (signed 'Path to car park') and cross Miresbeck for

the last time. This takes you down a track between a campsite and Glenridding Beck. As you walk along the bank, notice the reinforcements on the far side.

Glenridding Beck is a spectacular torrent after a thaw and the embankments are vital in spring. The most dramatic flooding came after a night of heavy rainfall on 30 October 1927. The dam at Kepple Cove burst, sending a quarter of a million gallons of water and 25,000 tons of rock and debris crashing into the valley. Many homes were washed away but incredibly no one was hurt, although there were newspaper reports of dramatic and heroic rescues. The debris from the flood spilled out into the lake and formed the promontory which now serves as the car park at the Ullswater steamer pier.

This is a very pleasant part of the walk which takes you along the tree-lined riverbank and brings you back to the outward path. Turn left and walk back into Glenridding.

VISITOR ATTRACTIONS
See Walk 22: Ullswater.

8 TARN HOWS

PARKING AND START/FINISH

The walk starts from the limited free parking off the road at Tom Gill, 400m (430yd) south of Yew Tree Tarn on the A593 (GR 323998). If cheating, use the National Trust pay-and-display car park at Tarn Hows

DISTANCE

4km (2½ miles)

TERRAIN

Apart from the moderate climb alongside Tom Gill, the walking is all very easy and level

This is a classic walk in one of the most popular spots in the Lake District. Tarn Hows is owned by the National Trust and the footpath around the tarn was refurbished in 1993 to provide a gentle, level stroll. It is ideal for older and younger legs – and for those in between who want a pleasant, undemanding walk. For the more adventurous, the route starts with a climb alongside Tom Gill. Those feeling less energetic can use the National Trust car park at Tarn Hows.

LOOKING north from the car park, the path heads straight into Lane Head Coppice beside the road, goes over a footbridge and then bears right to start climbing. Dogs can be let off the lead almost immediately.

The path climbs alongside Tom Gill. There are occasional paths into the woods, which are mostly diversions. The river bends to the left and you can see a stone wall and field on the opposite bank. A path then comes in from the right but you should keep to the riverbank as far as another fork. Go right, climbing alongside a narrow ravine and past a small waterfall. Note that at the end of a long summer, this is a raging torrent of damp moss. Continue along the river to a kissing gate in a wire fence. Go through the gate and walk upstream to join the main path at Tarn Hows. Turn left and follow the yellow brick road around the tarn.

This area consisted originally of a number of smaller tarns, called Monk Coniston Tarns. In the 1850s the outflow was dammed by James Marshall of Monk Coniston Farm, to make a larger tarn and provide power for a local saw mill. Tarn Hows has been in the possession of the National Trust since 1930, and a survey conducted in 1974 estimated that around 750,000 people visit the tarn each year. However, it also revealed that only 10 per cent of them actually walk around the tarn. That's still an average of over 200 a day, so the only time you are likely to get the place to yourself is in the depths of winter around, say, three o'clock in the morning.

After about 200m (220yd) the path forks. Keep right, following the path around the head of the tarn. The route is very easy to follow and very little description is required here. When in doubt, bear

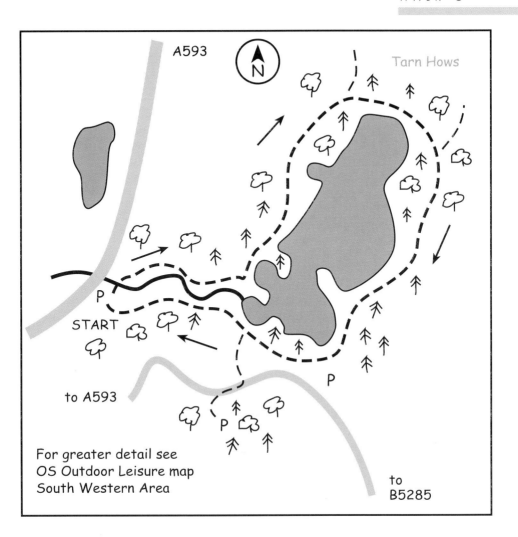

right and keep close to the tarn. At the head of the tarn the path veers away to lead you through a very wide kissing gate and then back into the trees.

Shortly after the kissing gate there is a path off left, through the stone wall, which goes across the moor to Arnside Intake. This is a pleasant diversion and considerably quieter. No one ever goes to Arnside Intake, so if you want somewhere quiet to eat your sandwiches this is a diversion well worth taking. After visiting the little tarn, retrace your steps and continue along the main path around Tarn Hows.

As you begin to approach the road again you will pass through a second large kissing gate, and the path then forks. Keep bearing right, staying as close to the water as you can, rather than going up to the road. This will bring you back to the main gate, by the dam

43

at Tom Gill. Do not go through the gate but instead turn left. There are two paths in front of you; the wide path goes to the car park, while the narrower, right-hand one climbs to a fallen tree trunk and a view of the tarn. Turn right along the trunk, and the route then heads off down a narrow path, away from the tarn and down through bracken. You will have a stone wall and the woods on your right-hand side.

As you drop down alongside the wall, you can see the path up through the woods on your right. The wall turns into a wire fence and then drops down to a derelict stone barn. Turn right, then where the path forks go straight, alongside an old wall and down to a wooden farm gate. Go through the gate and turn right down an unmade vehicle track. This takes you straight back to the car park and the start of the walk.

VISITOR ATTRACTIONS

Beatrix Potter Gallery
Main Street, Hawkshead
Tel: 015394 35355
A small museum in the old solicitor's offices which belonged to William
Heelis, Beatrix Potter's husband. The exhibition tells the story of Beatrix
Potter herself rather than her books, and includes her exquisite plant
paintings.

Hill Top, Near Sawrey, Windermere
Tel: 015394 36269
Beatrix Potter's famous Lake District home, a place of pilgrimage for fans
from all over the world.

For attractions in Coniston see Walk 13: Levers Water & Church Beck.

*Tom Gill winds
through Lane
Head Coppice,
on the way to
Tarn Hows*

9 STANLEY FORCE & RIVER ESK

PARKING AND START/FINISH

The walk starts from the National Park Authority car park at Trough House (GR 172003). Driving west from Hardknott to Ravenglass, it is the first turning left after Dalegarth railway station (about 300m (325yd) beyond the station). This is an isolated car park, so ensure all valuables are hidden from view

DISTANCE
4.2km (2½ miles)

TERRAIN
A level walk to the first of the bridges over Stanley Ghyll, thereafter progressively steeper with some potentially slippery rock. The short section above the final bridge is optional and should be tackled with caution in wet weather. The walk back along the Esk is level and easy

Stanley Force is not the Lake District's longest waterfall, but its setting in a deep, wooded gorge makes it one of the most picturesque and dramatic. This is a short walk which combines the falls with a stroll along the Esk, a strong candidate for the title of Cumbria's prettiest river.

TURN left out of the car park and follow the unmade lane past the entrance to Dalegarth Hall. Go through a wooden farm gate and past two field gates. This is a crossroads of walks: the left is signed 'Boot and Upper Eskdale', the right 'Eskdale Green'. Continue past the gates (signed 'Stanley Ghyll' and 'Birker Fell'), and as the lane curves right there is a pair of wooden gates in the stone wall on your left. Once through you are into the national park Stanley Ghyll Access Area (signed 'Waterfalls').

Walk straight ahead and you will come to the river. Turn right and follow the river upstream. The riverside footpath is clear and easy to follow and leads you through a mature mixed woodland. This has been heavily planted in the past and the gorge wall is a mass of thick vegetation, dominated by large rhododendrons. After a few hundred metres the sides of the gorge start to close in. When you arrive at the first wooden footbridge, you will see the rock face of the gorge wall ahead of you. The bridge looks as though it might present exciting possibilities – the far side appears to be perched on a pile of stones – so carry on across.

Continue up the far bank, beginning to climb. The wall above you is thick with ferns and rhododendrons and the rocks are covered in moss. After about 80m (85yd) you will come to the second bridge and, once across, will need to climb a set of steps cut in the rock. At the top of the steps the path splits. You will be coming back to this point, so for the time being head straight on, dropping temporarily to the third bridge. You can now glimpse Stanley Force plummeting down within the cleft ahead. The skyline ahead is a narrow V-shape as the sides of the gorge rise above you. The roar of water is loud and the atmosphere is tremendously fresh and invigorating.

Halfway across the third bridge is a stile and a notice which

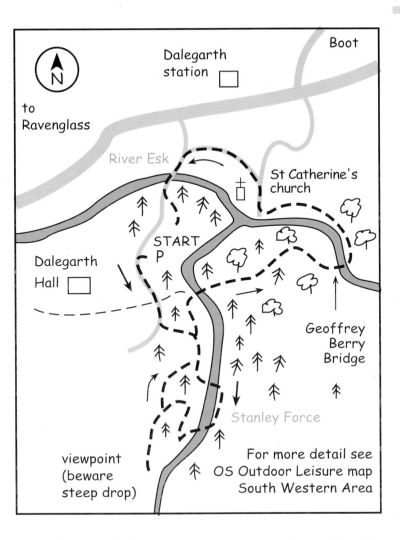

Boot

Dalegarth
station

to
Ravenglass

River Esk

St Catherine's
church

START
P

Dalegarth
Hall

Geoffrey
Berry
Bridge

Stanley Force

viewpoint
(beware
steep drop)

For more detail see
OS Outdoor Leisure map
South Western Area

warns that the path ahead is steep and slippery. In heavy rainfall the next section can be tricky, but at other times it is safe enough if taken carefully. Once over the bridge you climb the side of the gorge for a further 50m (54yd) or so to a splendid view of Stanley Force. The ghyll plunges 11m (36ft) into a dark pool overhung by vegetation. Notice the tree trunk which spans the gorge above the falls.

The path ends here; a fence and sign just below this viewpoint make it clear that this is the limit of public access. However, there is an additional view of the waterfall. Retrace your way to the top of the steps between the second and third bridge, and then follow the handrails (rather than dropping down to the second bridge). They will lead you up the side of the gorge, following a second beck upstream. As the path levels off, there is a slate footbridge over the beck. Cross the beck and go up the hill, past a sign which

47

*Stanley Ghyll
makes its way
between moss-
covered rocks
and mixed
woodland*

warns '150ft sheer drop, rock viewing platform 150 yards'. The path leads a short distance through the trees to a metal fence and the top of the rock crag. Put dogs on leads and hold children by the hand as you approach this. From the top of the crag you peer straight down into the gorge for another view of the waterfall. It is a good view but not as spectacular as the one from below, so don't feel you have missed out if you decide to hold back. Incidentally, there is a stile at the end of the metal fence. Crossing into the field, you can work your way over the top of the river to another view-point on the opposite side of the gorge – you can see it from the rock platform – but the view is disappointing. There is so much vegetation that the waterfall is hidden from view.

Retrace your steps to the slate footbridge, then continue straight up the wooded hillside on the other side. The path winds around the hill, on the side away from the gorge, and drops down through the trees towards a stone wall. The path then forks, the left-hand option going down to a farm gate. Ignore this and go right, and the path will take you back to the outward route, beside the river. When you reach the point where you joined the path, at the entrance to the woods, continue along the bank until you come to a wooden footbridge. Cross over it and leave the woods via a farm gate.

The path goes three ways. Bear left across the field and the path will lead you through the oak trees to the River Esk. This is a very pretty river, with its banks overhung by rowan and birch. Turn right along the bank, heading upstream. You will pass the stepping stones to the church on the far bank. These are usually slippery and often under water, so don't try to cross here. Continue along the bank for a few more minutes and you will enter a small gorge and arrive at a wooden footbridge.

The bridge was built in 1990 as a memorial to Lakeland writer and photographer, Geoffrey Berry. A dedicated campaigner for Lakeland conservation, Geoffrey was secretary of the Friends of the Lake District for 10 years from 1966. He was consultant secretary from 1976 until his death in 1988, at the age of 75. He wrote several books, notably A Tale of Two Lakes, *which told the story of the Friends' campaign to prevent North West Water and British Nuclear Fuels Limited extracting water from Wast Water and Ennerdale Water. He was awarded the OBE in 1977 in recognition of his conservation work. The Geoffrey Berry bridge was designed and built by the National Park Authority and National Trust, the £5000 cost funded entirely from donations.*

Geoffrey's photographs appeared in numerous books and in the Victoria & Albert Museum. His pictures illustrated my first book, so I always remember him as I walk this part of the Esk.

Look underneath the bridge and you'll see that it is supported by two steel girders – all that remains of the branch line which once carried iron ore from the nearby mine to the Eskdale railway at Boot. Until the bridge was built, walkers crossing the gorge required strong nerves and a good sense of balance.

You can explore further along the tree-lined bank, but this side is a dead end. Cross the gated bridge and walk back along the bank towards the church. You will go through a kissing gate and after 100m (110yd) arrive at St Catherine's church.

St Catherine's Church dates from the seventeenth century and is built on the site of an earlier chapel. There is a particularly interesting memorial in the churchyard to Tommy Dobson. He was the founder and master of the Eskdale and Ennerdale foxhounds and in his day was as famous as Caldbeck's John Peel (of the song 'D'ye ken John Peel?'). Dobson was a bobbin turner by trade and when he died on 2 April 1910 this stone memorial was erected by 'nearly 300 friends from all parts of the country'.

Turn right to a farm gate and, once through, go left along the track between the stone walls (signed 'Public bridleway'). This route takes you back alongside the river to the road. At the road, turn left over the bridge. The view from here can be entertaining in summer. The river is quite deep and there are often various noisy characters swinging off ropes and diving into the pools. It is also a favourite spot for scuba enthusiasts on practice dives.

Just across the bridge, you have a choice. You can either follow the road back to the car park, or you can cheat. To do this, look for the narrow gap in the stone wall on your left. This is a variety of stile known locally as 'fat man's agony'. Squeeze through and walk straight up the gentle, wooded hill back to the car park.

Further upstream is a stone packhorse bridge, known as Doctor Bridge. You can extend the walk to include the bridge; for a suggested route, see my Walker's Companion: Lake District *(Ward Lock, 1994). The bridge was widened in 1734 so that the local doctor, Edward Tyson, could take his pony and trap across.*

VISITOR ATTRACTIONS

Eskdale Corn Mill
Boot, Eskdale
Tel: 019467 23335
A converted corn mill, which is no longer working but has a good display on the history and technology.

Muncaster Castle
Muncaster, Ravenglass
Tel: 01229 717203
Originally a pele tower, now a large mansion set in magnificent grounds overlooking the Esk estuary. Famous for rhododendrons and azaleas, there is also a small zoo and the British Owl Breeding and Release Centre.

Muncaster Mill
Muncaster, Ravenglass
Tel: 01229 717232
A working corn mill in regular use, and one of the stops for the
Ravenglass and Eskdale Railway. Freshly produced flour is available.

Ravenglass & Eskdale Railway
Ravenglass
Tel: 01229 717171
'La'al Ratty' to the locals, this narrow-gauge railway was once a mining
line but is now run for the benefit of passengers – not only a useful
service, but a brilliant attraction in its own right.

Opposite: *A quiet
spot on the River
Esk below Gill
Force*

Left: *Tommy
Dobson's grave
in St Catherine's
churchyard. In
his day, the
founder and
master of the
Eskdale and
Ennerdale fox-
hounds was as
famous as
Caldbeck's John
Peel*

10 RIVER GRETA

The River Greta winds its way along a spectacular river gorge, once traversed by the Cockermouth to Penrith railway. Now the railway line is disused and, in an excellent example of creative park management, has been turned into an easy, level walking route. After walking the line, the return is via Brundholme Woods, along the side of the steep river gorge. This is an ideal walk for families and hardy, mountaineering types who fancy a day off.

THE start of this walk is wonderfully straightforward: from the station platform, simply set off down the track.

It's a great shame that the station itself has been allowed to become so derelict. It ought to be a museum, café or information centre, extolling the virtues and history of the surrounding area. Fortunately, the track itself is in excellent condition: a broad, flat, tree-lined route which very quickly brings you to the first of the bridges and a view of the river. As you cross, notice the iron railway girders under the bridge. On the far side, the steps on the left lead to the Keswick Bridge timeshare development. You will be returning up these later.

Rail transport arrived in Keswick in 1864, with the building of the Penrith to Cockermouth railway. Designed to finish the link between the ore fields of the west coast and industry in the north east of England, the line cost £267,000 for just over 50km (31 miles) of track, including 135 bridges. The line followed the present route of the A66, hugging the western shore of Bassenthwaite Lake. It must have been a magnificent line to travel – imagine sitting in a carriage, eating your nineteenth-century breakfast and watching Blencathra and Skiddaw speeding past the window. The Penrith to Cockermouth line closed in June 1972.

The track continues through the outskirts of Keswick, passing a row of council houses and the sports field and then under a grey slate road bridge. The track narrows at this point and you approach the A66 flyover, which spans the river valley via four magnificent arches. As you pass through the two gates, look along the length of the flyover and notice the sweeping curve of the arch. You will also

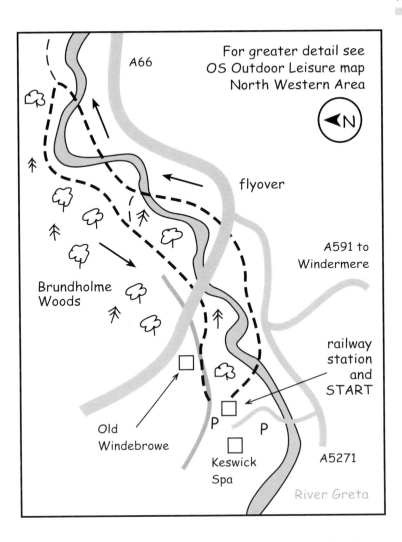

A66

For greater detail see
OS Outdoor Leisure map
North Western Area

◄N

flyover

A591 to
Windermere

Brundholme
Woods

railway
station
and
START

Old
Windebrowe

P   P

Keswick
Spa

A5271

River Greta

notice the thump and rumble of the lorries passing overhead.

The path leaves the line of the track at this point to climb up to
the main road. Put dogs on leads for this bit. As you reach the road,
the path swings downhill again via a short flight of steps, back
towards the river. The conifer-covered fell on the far side of the
river valley is Latrigg. As you descend you will get a surprising
view of the river, the wide, tree-lined gorge and the weir below.
You will drop down to rejoin the line of the track and then walk
upstream alongside the Greta. This must have been a dramatic train
ride. The track is nearly 10m (33ft) above the level of the river, giving you an unparalleled view of the 50m (162ft) wide gorge. You
will pass under another narrow bridge into a cutting and then
arrive at a railway platform. This is Low Briery and there is disabled
access here to the track from the nearby caravan site.

🔊 *Low Briery is the site of one of the 20 bobbin mills operating in the Lake District in the mid-nineteenth century, which was a time when the area supplied 50 per cent of worldwide demand from the cotton industry. Low Briery's 40 million bobbins a year were exported as far afield as Hong Kong, Uruguay and South Africa. The mill ceased production in 1961.*

Shortly after you emerge from the cutting, the Greta makes another loop and the track goes over magnificent 80m (85yd) long bridge. Just on the far side a set of steps leads into the woods, providing a way of shortening the walk if necessary. About 150m (163yd) further along the track the river bends again, so you have to cross over another bridge. The track is several metres above the surrounding woodland and this section of the walk is very pretty.

Below: *One of
the old railway
bridges over the
River Greta*

Above: *The River
Greta seen from
the path through
Brundholme
Woods*

Just beyond the bridge, look out for the square box on your left. This is an old grit box, used for scattering lime on the track in winter. A few metres on there is a stile in the wire fence on your left. If you are feeling adventurous, you can cross into the woods and walk along the riverbank to the next bridge. There are a couple of benches along the way, the second one marked in memory of Alf Price, from members of the Keswick Angler's Association.

Keeping to the track, you will come to the most picturesque of the bridges: a suspended, 40m (43yd) long structure and the last for this route. The railway line carries on for another 3km (2 miles) to Threlkeld village and you can link it with a walk beside the River Glenderamackin. But for now, turn left after the bridge and cross the stile into a field (signed 'Keswick via Brundholme Woods'). Climb up the steep bank and over another stile, and you are into Brundholme Woods.

The path leads downstream along the steep side of the river gorge. You climb 71 log steps and then arrive at a T-junction. Turn left here (signed 'Keswick'). The path winds its way through the woods following the contours of the hill, crossing a number of pretty becks and keeping in view of the river throughout. At times, the side of the hill drops away very steeply to the river, some 20m (65ft) below.

Eventually the path drops to the level of the river, and after 1km (⅔ mile) or so you can see the line of the railway track on the far bank. The path leads past a small, dark conifer plantation and brings you back to the A66 flyover – from this bank you get an even better view of it. On the far side of the river at this point is a collection of buildings which once housed the local saw mill.

The path ends at a gate and a flight of steps. The gate leads you on to a tarmac lane beside a small bridge. The permissive path, however, goes right, up the steps and back up the riverbank. Follow the path through the woods and it will bring you to Old Windebrowe and the Calvert Trust riding stables.

William and Dorothy Wordsworth lived here at Old Windebrowe in 1794, shortly after William's sojourn to France. The sixteenth-century farmhouse was owned by William Calvert and Wordsworth was nursing his brother, Raisley, through a terminal illness. When Raisley died, he bequeathed William enough money to concentrate on a career as a poet. The house is now owned by the Calvert Trust, which provides riding and outdoor activities for the disabled. Two rooms are open to the public.

Walk through the stable grounds to the minor road and turn left. After 50m (54yd) you will come to a sign pointing left ('Footpath to Keswick'). You could follow the lane back to the railway station car park, but for a more interesting route go left here, doubling back along the drive to Brundholme Country House. As you come to the house, there is another path off to the right (signed 'Footpath to Keswick'). This leads you into the rhododendron bushes alongside a field and gives you another good view of Latrigg.

Cross over a bridge and the path then leads into the grounds of Keswick Bridge timeshare. As you drop down towards the road, you can see the Keswick Hotel on your left. At the road, go left and up the steps to rejoin the railway walk. Turn right and you're back at the station.

VISITOR ATTRACTIONS

Keswick Museum
Fitz Park, Keswick
Tel: 017687 73263
One of Cumbria's oldest museums, full of oddities. Contains a collection of original manuscripts from Southey and the Lake poets, and features a small art gallery.

Cumberland Pencil Museum
Southey Works, Keswick
Tel: 017687 73626
The history of pencil making, from the discovery of graphite in the fells of Borrowdale to the world's largest pencil, a Guinness Record-holder. Good fun for children of all ages.

Cars of the Stars Museum
Standish Street, Keswick
Tel: 017687 73757
A museum which appeals to car and film buffs alike. Contains original vehicles from films and television series such as *Chitty Chitty, Bang, Bang, James Bond, Batman, Knight Rider* and *Back to the Future*.

Beatrix Potter's Lake District
Packhouse Court, Keswick
Tel: 015394 35599
An exhibition about the National Trust and its connections with Beatrix Potter, who bequeathed the Trust her 15 farms, 4000 acres of land and numerous flocks of Herdwick sheep.

The Calvert Trust
Old Windebrowe, Keswick
Tel: 017687 72112
Provides horse riding and outdoor facilities for the disabled. The Calvert Trust can be also contacted at their headquarters at Little Crosthwaite, Under Skiddaw. Tel: 017687 72254.

11 RIVER DERWENT

This river walk is one of my favourites. Despite being in the heart of the most rugged of the Lakeland dales, the walk is a gentle stroll through woods alongside a wonderfully clear and quick-moving river. It is followed by an ascent along one of the ancient packhorse routes and then a swift descent through fields, with magnificent views across the valley to Rosthwaite and the mountains beyond.

Leaving the car park, turn right and follow the narrow lane away from the centre of the village. You will pass several pretty stone cottages and come to a fork in the road at Yew Tree Farm. Go right, over the cobbled farmyard (signed 'Footpath to Grange') and along a rough farm track between fields. If it is the right time of year, look out for the sheep-shearing pens on the right.

The track swings right at the river and leads you to a new-looking packhorse bridge – notice the way the stonework has been constructed. The last tree on the left, before the bridge, is a rather nice pollarded willow. Once across the bridge, turn right along the track to a pair of farm gates. Go through the right-hand gate and keep to the riverbank. The Derwent is very powerful when in spate, washing stones and small boulders out into the

The New Bridge over the River Derwent features some interesting stonework

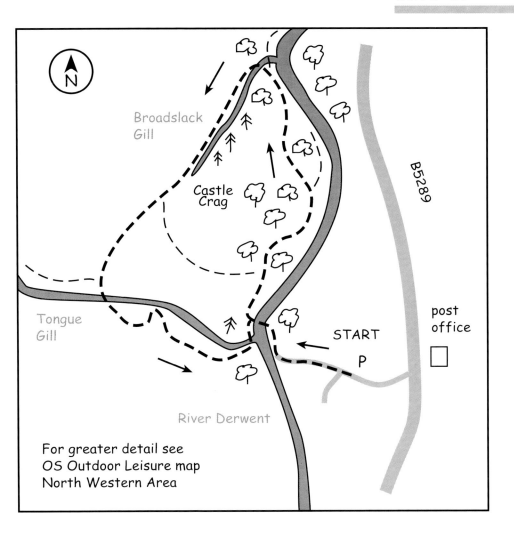

Broadslack
Gill

Castle
Crag

B5289

Tongue
Gill

post
office

START

P

River Derwent

For greater detail see
OS Outdoor Leisure map
North Western Area

surrounding fields, and you can see the embankments where the riverbank has been reinforced.

The track crosses a beck and winds around a small knoll, leading to High Hows Wood. Once through the kissing gate you will find yourself in a lovely old mixed woodland, the trees on your left rising up the lower flanks of Castle Crag.

Unlikely though it seems, Borrowdale is named after Castle Crag. The 290m (943ft) summit was a hill fort over 2000 years ago. It is in an ideal position, strategically placed where the valley narrows and the mountains rise precipitously on either side – known to the early, eighteenth-century tourists as the Jaws of Borrowdale. Roman and Samarian pottery has been found on the site, but the remains of the hill fort have long since destroyed by quarrying. Castle Crag was given to the National Trust in 1920 by Sir William Hamer and there is a memorial plaque to him on a seat, visible as you climb the crag. And the name? Borrowdale comes from the old Norse word borgarárdalr – *the valley of the fort.*

After crossing two small becks, the path appears to split. The right fork takes you for a lovely grassy stroll along the riverbank – a delightful way to examine the blue pools and rocks and the mysterious ox-bow bends. This feels like real exploration and is great for kids. Unfortunately, it is also a dead end: a moss-covered rock outcrop blocks the route. (I'm not recommending this, but if you have a head for heights it is possible to climb the sloping back of the rock for a tremendous and unusual view of the surrounding valley, standing above the tree tops. The photographer got very excited when we discovered this view and promptly lost a lens cap.)

Back on the main path, you continue through the woods to the quarry. The path winds past a large cairn, built from the slate rubble which covers the fellside just here. Beyond the slate tip the path climbs to a T-junction. Go right, downhill between two rocks, through a stone wall and out of the woods. Turn right again and follow the path downhill.

♪ Stone was quarried in this area until the 1930s. It was also the home of an eccentric mountaineer named Millican Dalton, who lived in a nearby cave and liked to be known as the Professor of Adventure. He was born in Alston in 1867 and worked as a shipping clerk in London, before effectively dropping out to return to the love of his life, the mountains. He was a mountain guide in Scotland, the Lakes and Switzerland, and spent the summer months living in his cave. He was vegetarian and made his own clothes, earning an income by giving lessons in climbing and raft building. A famous photograph of him aboard his home-built raft, Rogue Herries, *was a bestselling postcard and can still be seen hanging on the wall in Keswick cafés. Dalton died in 1947, but if you search for it you can still find his cave. It has an idiosyncratic inscription above the entrance: 'Don't!! waste words, or jump to conclusions.'*

The path leads to a broad track. Continue straight on and you will rejoin the river. This is another lovely stretch of the walk. The river is very broad and deep along here and in summer it is a good spot for swimming. It's a pity about the noise from the road on the far bank.

Continue over a stile and the path drops to a wooden footbridge over Broadslack Gill, which feeds into the Derwent at this point. At the signpost, turn left ('Seatoller, Honister') up a stony path, leaving the River Derwent behind. You are now following an ancient packhorse route.

♪ Packhorse routes cross the Lake District, connecting the major dales and providing trading routes. Many of these date back to the twelfth century, when wool had to be transported from the farms

*owned by Furness Abbey, near Barrow-in-Furness, and Fountains
Abbey in Yorkshire. The routes continued to be used into the nineteenth century until the road networks became established and, later,
railways were developed.*

The packhorse route climbs the fell, crossing the river every now
and again. Once you emerge from the woods, Goat Crag makes an
impressive skyline on your right. Keep straight on, ignoring the
path to the left which climbs Castle Crag. As you cross the beck for
the final time and arrive at a group of three sheep pens, there is a
superb view of Glaramara ahead of you. Stop and turn around for
an even better view, taking in Derwent Water, Skiddaw and the distinctive volcano shape of Castle Head, the hill to the right of the
lake. Castle Head really is the remains of an old volcano. It's a
superb viewpoint and there is a viewfinder on top which names
the surrounding mountains.

About 100m (110yd) from the sheep pens there is a marker
post and the path splits. Go left down the narrower path, which
takes you to the wooden footbridge over Tongue Gill. As you walk
down, the view on the left opens up and you can see across the
fields to Rosthwaite and Watendlath fell. Tongue Gill can be a raging torrent after heavy rainfall and is very impressive, yet this is a
comparatively little-known route, most walkers preferring to come
down closer to Castle Crag.

Cross the two footbridges to the gate and stile. About 30m
(33yd) beyond the stile, a farm track crosses the path. Turn left
down the track to the wooden farm gate. Once through the gate
the track leads down a steep field, which can be slippery and
muddy after heavy rain. The track meanders somewhat – if in
doubt, keep Rosthwaite directly ahead of you. You can see the
River Derwent below, winding across the pattern of fields.

The track takes you past a stone wall (and a sign pointing right
to 'Scale Close Coppice and Seatoller') and down to a stile in the
far right-hand corner of the field beside Tongue Gill. Cross over the
stile and footbridge and then continue across two more fields,
keeping to the riverbank. Eventually you will come to a final stile
as Tongue Gill joins the River Derwent. Once over the stile, there
are two footbridges in front of you. Go right if you want to explore
the opposite bank to the outward part of the trip (but be warned
that you have to ford the river to get back to Rosthwaite).
Alternatively, cross the left-hand footbridge and the path will take
you back to New Bridge. Turn right over the bridge and follow the
track back to the starting point.

VISITOR ATTRACTIONS

For attractions in Keswick see Walk 10: River Greta.

12 EASEDALE TARN

PARKING AND START/FINISH
The walk starts from the small pay-and-display car park at the top of Easedale Road (the lane beside the Heaton Cooper Gallery). Alternatively, use the National Park Authority car park in the village, just north of the shops on the B5287

DISTANCE
7.5km (4¾ miles), including the 1.5km (1 mile) circuit of the tarn

TERRAIN
Straightforward walking for the most part, with a steep climb to Easedale Tarn and some rough ground during the descent

Although Easedale Tarn is isolated in the fells above Grasmere, it is easy to reach from the village. It is a popular walk for beginner fell walkers, with a real feel of being in the mountains. This route begins in Far Easedale, allowing you to enjoy the peace and quiet before climbing to Easedale Tarn and encountering the crowds who have ascended from Grasmere.

WALK along Easedale Road, away from the village centre. Opposite the car park there is a stile and a short section of permissive footpath which takes you off the road. You rejoin the road at Goody Bridge, and just past the farm the road swings right. The footbridge in the trees on your right will be used on the return route, so don't be tempted by the sign to 'Easedale Tarn'. Continue along the road, past Lancrigg Hotel, and it will take you across a field, with the sharp pinnacle of Helm Crag directly ahead of you. This has a couple of alternative names derived from the silhouettes formed by the craggy summit: The Lion and the Lamb can be seen from Dunmail Raise, while from Easedale Tarn it becomes The Old Lady at the Organ. Heap of Old Rocks doesn't seem to have caught the local imagination.

Once past a small cluster of houses (including the engagingly named Little Parrock), you will come to a fork. Go right (signed 'Far Easedale and Helm Crag') on to a rough track, which leads up to a metal farm gate. Go through the gate (ignoring the sign on your right which lures you off to the 'Wordsworth memorial and hikers' tea barn') and then bear left to another fork in the path. Go left here (signed 'Far Easedale and Borrowdale').

♪ *There are a number of very long-established trading routes which link the valleys, and once you get on the tops it is easy to lose your way and come down in the wrong place. Friends of mine at a local guest house occasionally rescue guests who set off walking to Langdale, come down in Borrowdale and are faced with an expensive taxi ride back to Grasmere.*

The path takes you between some fine examples of drystone walls and across a number of fields. It is an easy route to follow. (One

64

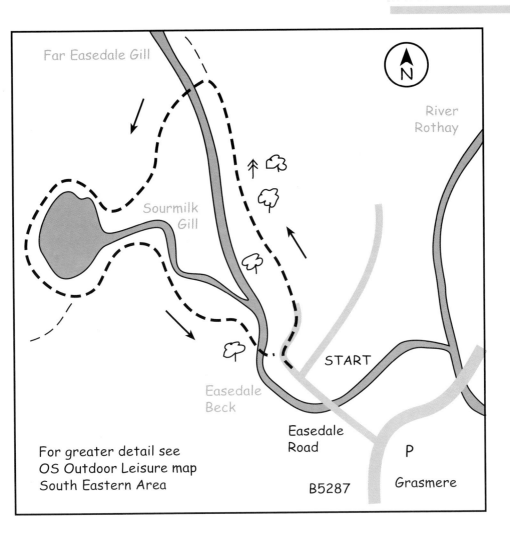

Far Easedale Gill

River
Rothay

N

Sourmilk
Gill

START

Easedale
Beck

Easedale
Road

P

For greater detail see
OS Outdoor Leisure map
South Eastern Area

B5287

Grasmere

intriguing point: who thought to plant a monkey puzzle tree out here in the middle of nowhere? It's by the field entrance, just before you reach two stone barns on your right.) This path feels very isolated. When you reach the stone barns, you can glance across the valley to see the swarm of dots heading up the more direct route to Easedale Tarn.

A few minutes' walk past the barns and you will reach Far Easedale Gill, which is a pleasant, bubbling companion as you follow it upstream. The path brings you to a long wooden footbridge. Cross over and you can see the footpath to Borrowdale winding across the fell ahead of you and disappearing into the head of the valley. About 40m (43yd) from the bridge, the path forks. Go left and climb steeply past a split boulder and a footpath marker.

The path climbs to the top of the field on your left: then, at

65

another pair of marker posts, it veers off to the right. Keep climbing, and after 10 minutes or so you will come to Sourmilk Gill and another view of the main path to the tarn. Keeping to your side of the gill, follow the path around the boggy bits. Dogs are very useful here as they tend to rush ahead and you can tell by the splashing noises which routes to avoid.

♤ Sourmilk (or Sour Milk) is a popular name: there are three Sour Milk Gills in the Lake District. And on the subject of nomenclature, 'gill' is derived from an old Norse word for a wooded valley containing a stream. Wordsworth popularized the spelling 'ghyll', which looks more romantic but is now going out of fashion.

This boggy section gets horribly wet in winter and there are occasional lines of stepping stones – not enough, however, so don't hesitate to abandon the path and climb to firmer ground when you need to. The path runs roughly parallel to the river, although this is out of view most of the time, concealed by the bracken. The path finally approaches the gill and then, suddenly, you arrive at Easedale Tarn.

♤ Easedale was well known to William and Dorothy Wordsworth when they lived at Dove Cottage in Grasmere. They called it 'the black quarter' because all the bad weather seemed to come from this direction. A local inn keeper built a refreshment hut by Easedale Tarn and sold teas, carried up in an urn. He even hired out a rowing boat. The hut was demolished in the 1960s and its remains now form the cairn on the far side of the river. A painting of the tarn and hut hangs in Dove Cottage.

Easedale tarn is very pretty, with impressive crags on three sides: from the left, these are Blea Crag, Slapestone Edge, Tarn Crag and Greathead Crag. There is usually a seagull perched on the rock in the centre. You could cross the beck and head straight downhill, but if it is relatively dry underfoot it is worth circling the tarn. Heading anti-clockwise, the perspective changes dramatically. As you reach the far side, the path climbs to avoid boggy sections and you should work your way up to a major footpath which continues out of Easedale and on to Stickle Tarn and the Langdales. Once you hit the path, turn left and follow the route back to Sourmilk Gill. The entire circuit takes about half an hour.

As you reach the gill, the path forks. Go right, or you could end up circling the tarn forever. After walking downhill for 20m (22yd) you will have a tremendous view of Helm Crag and Grasmere, with Fairfield on the far side of the valley. The route downhill is fairly straightforward, although rough underfoot in places. After 15 minutes or so you will come to the first of the cascades in Sourmilk Gill. The rock pools just below are excellent for a paddle on a hot summer's day.

66

The path drops down to a stone wall and goes through a kissing gate, and then joins a farm track across the fields. Keep to the track, through an ornate metal farm gate and across another field. At the far side, over a concrete bridge, there are two farm gates. Go through the left-hand gate and back alongside Easedale Beck. The path leads you into the woods and across a footbridge, and you are then back at Easedale Road by the Lancrigg Hotel. Turn right and seek out one of the tea shops in the village.

A dramatic view of Easedale, with Tarn Crag in the background

VISITOR ATTRACTIONS

Heaton Cooper Studio
Grasmere
Tel: 015394 35280
A small gallery selling cards, prints and paintings by the Heaton Cooper family.

For further attractions, see Walk 20: Rydal Water & Grasmere.

13 LEVERS WATER & CHURCH BECK

PARKING AND START/FINISH
The walk starts from the National Park Authority car park in the centre of Coniston village, on the B5285 (follow signs for the tourist information centre)

DISTANCE
7.5km (4¾ miles)

TERRAIN
A long climb to Levers Water, with some sections of rough track. The circuit of Levers Water may be wet and boggy in places. An easy descent

Levers Water stands in a natural cove, on the side of the Old Man of Coniston. Once a natural tarn, it has been dammed and enlarged to provide power for the mining operations in Coppermines Valley. This route ascends alongside the Levers Waterfall, circles the tarn and comes down via Boulder Valley and Church Beck. Although it is hard going in places, you are rewarded with wonderful views of Coniston and the chance to explore a landscape rich in industrial heritage.

FROM the centre of the village, head down Yewdale Road and turn left opposite the post office, up a cul-de-sac between the Black Bull Hotel and the Co-Op store. The road runs alongside Church Beck and you will quickly find yourself out of the village and surrounded by fields, heading towards Wetherlam and Long Crag.

The road narrows to a single, rough track and is signed 'Coppermines Youth Hostel'. (Note the warning sign for quarries and mines. There are a number of deep shafts in Coppermines Valley – do not be tempted to go caving.) The lane climbs gradually uphill, and once over the cattle grid you will start to get a view back to Coniston Water. The white house on the far shore is Brantwood, the home of John Ruskin.

Brantwood was the home of art critic, philosopher and social reformer John Ruskin. He lived here from 1872 to 1900, having bought the house sight unseen for £1500. He transformed a run-down property into a beautiful home and lived here for 30 years, until his death. The house is now open to the public and in recent years, with the help of European Union grants, the grounds have been restored to Ruskin's original layout. A fascinating place, it must occupy one of the most beautiful sites in Britain.

Once past the wood on your left, you get another view of the river and a small waterfall. Just above is Millers Bridge, a good viewpoint. Even better, scramble down and see how this old packhorse bridge has been constructed.

Continue up the track past another waterfall and you will see the white youth hostel ahead. The path forks: keep straight ahead, towards the hostel. Levers Water Beck on your left is very wide and

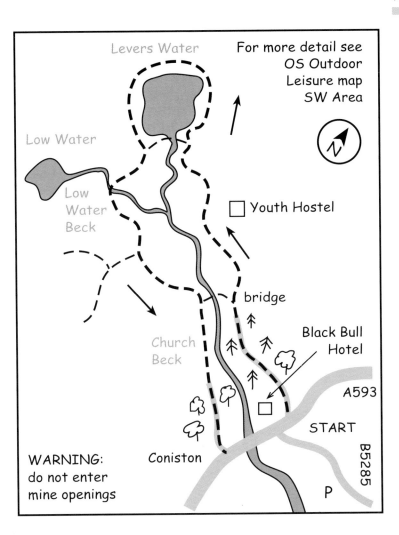

Levers Water

For more detail see
OS Outdoor
Leisure map
SW Area

N

Low Water

Low
Water
Beck

☐ Youth Hostel

bridge

Black Bull
Hotel

Church
Beck

A593

☐

START

WARNING:
do not enter
mine openings

Coniston

B5285

P

meanders through a valley wrecked by mining. Vegetation is reclaiming the spoil heaps, but it is still a desolate view. Another beck comes in from the right and across that you can see a terrace of houses, once miners' cottages and now used by the Yorkshire Mountaineering Club.

Copper has been mined from the Old Man of Coniston since Roman times. In the seventeenth century the German engineers of the Company of Mines Royal dug the area, and the copper ore was sent for smelting to the newly built smelting works at Keswick. The mines were at their peak in the 1850s, when 3000 tons of copper pyrite were dug out of the mountain each year, the shafts descending over 300m (1000ft). These were the most important copper mines in Europe, employing over 900 men. Mining declined when pumping water out of the deep shafts became uneconomic, and the mines finally closed

*in 1915. Coppermines Youth Hostel was once the home and office of
the mines manager.*

The track bears left, to pass in front of the youth hostel and alongside Levers Water Beck. Look out for the old mining carts scattered
about the valley floor. There is an information panel just past the
youth hostel; attempts have been made to establish a museum here
but so far the plans have always fallen foul of planning regulations.

Just past a stone hut (the old powder store for the mine) you
pass another waterfall, and in the hills to the left you can see Low
Water Beck tumbling down the fellside. Ahead is the Old Man of
Coniston and behind you can still see Coniston Water. Above the
waterfall the path forks, the left-hand option heading down to a
rusty iron footbridge. Go right, uphill, leaving the beck behind but
climbing towards Levers Waterfall. As you climb you will get a view
over the desolate foreground to Coniston Water and the pine-

*Levers Water Beck
in Coppermines
Valley, backed by
the Old Man of
Coniston*

Boulder Valley at dawn, looking towards the Old Man of Coniston

covered fells beyond. The track now begins to converge with the river once again. After a few minutes' steady climb, you will arrive at a small plateau and a crossroads in the path. The left turn leads to a wooden footbridge but you should go right, zigzagging up the hill past a small cave and an open mine shaft. The path gets steeper and is rough underfoot. As you approach the waterfall and the wall of the dam, look back for a brilliant view of Coniston Water, beyond that the Yorkshire Dales and, around to the right, Morecambe Bay. The tower on the hill just in front of the bay is the Barrow Monument at Ulverston, a replica of Eddystone Lighthouse.

Climb up to the dam wall and you will have arrived at Levers Water. About 38m (125ft) deep and surrounded on three sides by Great Crag, Little Crag and Erin Crag, Levers Water is a natural tarn but was dammed and the level raised in order to provide power for the copper mines.

You now have a choice. You could turn left, cross the river and begin dropping down almost immediately. A more interesting option is to make the 1.5km (1 mile) circuit anti-clockwise around the reservoir. Skirting the shore, the perspective changes continually, and with it the atmosphere of this isolated mountain tarn. The crags form a natural amphitheatre and you can hear the voices of walkers as they climb Gill Cove Crag on the far shore.

The path around the tarn is distinct until you reach Swirl Hawse Beck, whereupon it disappears into a bog. Go right down to the shore and you should be able to traverse the rocks and keep your boots dry. Looking back from this point, the solitary rock in the tarn acts as a sight, centred on the view into the valley below. Two-thirds of the way round the shore becomes very squelchy. Climb above the bog and you will join a path coming in from the right. Go left and follow the shore towards the dam.

The path is distinct as you enter a boulder field (this whole area is known as Boulder Valley) and approach a spoil tip on the right. Continue below the tip and a path will come in from the right, about 40m (43yd) before the dam wall. Turn right, back up this path, to climb the spoil tip and pass the mine opening on the left. This is a mine shaft which has collapsed and left a gaping hole in the hillside. There is a danger sign and the mine entrance is fenced off. Continue up the hill past a second fence and then bear left uphill: don't continue straight on or you will end up on the scree. Climb to the saddle between a grassy knoll on your left and the scree on your right, passing a large, flat-topped boulder. Looking back, you will get a final view of Levers Water.

Once over the saddle and you will drop down into the grassy valley, with a superb view of Coniston Water as you descend (watch out for *Gondola,* the National Trust steam launch). The grassy slope is littered with boulders and the path zigzags between them, heading towards Low Water Beck below. The view to the left opens up and you can see Coppermines Valley and the youth hostel once more. As you drop down to the beck there is a large, angular boulder on the left which looks like something imported from Easter Island. This is good for a practice scramble. Once across the beck, there is the remains of an old pipeline on the right and another huge boulder, frequently covered in rock climbers.

The path continues across the flanks of the Old Man, crossing another beck and then on to scree. You will pass a picturesque mine entrance on the right, with water dripping down the moss-covered rock. It is safe to peer in, but do not enter. The path continues below a crag and then reaches a T-junction with a much larger track. Turn left and walk downhill. After 20m (22yd), the track bears right around the hill and forks. Go straight on, downhill towards the youth hostel, to a gate in a stone wall. Go through this and walk across the field to a gap in another stone wall. The path bears left, away from the wall, to continue downhill through the bracken.

The path drops eventually to a wire fence. Follow it down the hill, alongside Levers Water Beck again, through another gate and down to Millers Bridge. You can cross over and retrace your steps to the car, or continue past the bridge without crossing and go through a kissing gate. The beck is now on the other side of a stone wall and you will drop down along the bottom of a field to a slate workshop. Once past the workshop, the path becomes a track and bears left, keeping to the river. You will cross another beck coming in from the right and then pass a lovely wooded spot by the river, complete with bench. This is a handy spot at which to sit and get your breath after the long slog down from Boulder Valley. Look carefully and you will be able to see railway signals in the woods on the far side of the beck. This is a private estate owned by a train enthusiast, who has built his own miniature line through the woods.

Continue down the track to arrive at Dixon Ground farm. Go through the gate on to the tarmac road and turn right. At the T-junction next to the Sun Inn, turn left and follow the road down to the village, emerging beside the road bridge in the centre of Coniston.

VISITOR ATTRACTIONS

Ruskin Museum
The Institute, Yewdale Road, Coniston
Tel: 015394 41541
A museum devoted to Ruskin, including correspondence, possessions and his geology collection. Also features a small exhibition about Donald Campbell.

Brantwood
Coniston
Tel: 015394 41396
Ruskin's home, open to the public in accordance with his wishes. There is an excellent nature trail around the grounds, and a range of events and exhibitions throughout the year. The Jumping Jenny café is excellent.

For details of the *Gondola,* Coniston Boating Centre and the Coniston Launches, see Walk 16: Coniston Water.

14 RIVER LOWTHER

PARKING AND START/FINISH
There is no car park in Askham but space can usually be found along the main street, where the walk starts

DISTANCE
8.5km (5¼ miles)

TERRAIN
An easy, Sunday afternoon type of stroll

Some of the nicest Cumbria countryside lies just outside the boundary of the national park. Less rugged and dramatic than the central Lakes, the area to the east of the park has superb river walks and a variety of delightful villages. This route explores the area around the village of Askham and the beautiful River Lowther, and offers a glimpse of what appear to be the gothic ruins of a castle.

WALKING down the centre of Askham village towards the river, look out for the lane on the left, opposite the Punchbowl Inn. It is by the boundary wall to Askham Hall, just below the village green. Turn along this lane, go through the studded wooden gates (signed 'Public bridleway') and walk along the track between two stone walls. You will catch sight of Askham Hall on your right.

🐾 *Unfortunately, Askham Hall is not accessible to the public. You get glimpses of this fine house from several points on the walk. Built in the fourteenth century as a pele tower, it was converted into an*

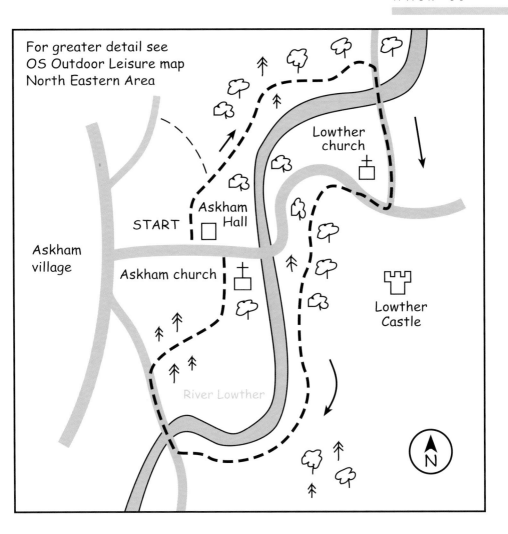

For greater detail see
OS Outdoor Leisure map
North Eastern Area

Lowther
church

Askham
Hall

START

Askham
village

Askham church

Lowther
Castle

River Lowther

N

*Elizabethan mansion in 1574 by Thomas Sandford and remained
in the Sandford family until 1828, when it became the rectory. It is
now the home of the Earl of Lonsdale, one of England's greatest
landowners. The name of the village, incidentally, means 'the place
with the ash trees'.*

The track goes past a barn and workshop to a farm gate. Go
through this and walk along the track between the fields. After
about 200m (220yd), look out for the footpath sign on your right.
Cross the stile and walk diagonally across the field to the far corner. A ladder stile takes you over the stone wall and into Heining
Wood. Like much of the woodland around here, this was planted
in the late 1950s and is part of the Lowther Estate. About 20m
(22yd) into the wood, you will come to a junction by a way-
marker post. Go left and the path will take you through the trees,

*Opposite: The
path through
Heining Wood*

just within the edge of the wood. You can hear the River Lowther somewhere through the trees to your right and you may catch a fleeting glimpse of Askham church.

The path narrows beside a short section of wooden rail (the ground slopes away steeply on your right) and, after another 200m (220yd) or so, you will begin to head downhill. When the path forks at the next rail, go right and keep a lookout for grouse scuttling through the undergrowth. You now drop down to walk alongside the River Lowther. This is a very pleasant stretch of woodland, and when you reach the metal gate it is tempting to carry straight on and continue walking along the tree-lined riverbank.

In fact, there is a right of way which allows you to continue along the river from this point. It runs through the woods for a further 3.25km (2 miles) to emerge near Penrith, at the exotically named King Arthur's Round Table (an early Bronze Age henge, although Sir Lancelot is rumoured to have killed a giant here). However, to make this a round trip involves 1.5km (1 mile) of road walking along the A6, breathing in a variety of fumes from heavy lorries, until you regain a footpath at the village of Clifton. The name Lowther is probably Old Norse (usually a safe bet in Cumbria) and comes from lauthra-a – *the foaming river.*

Go through the metal gate and you will find yourself on a tarmac lane running through the woods. Nip straight across for a short diversion, and from the splendid vantage point of the riverbank you can examine the stone bridge over the River Lowther. (The original bridge is no longer able to carry vehicles, so a lower, metal bridge has been built alongside.) Then go back up to the tarmac lane and cross the stone bridge via the stiles at either end. (These stiles are among the widest I have encountered, and were obviously designed for the efficient throughput of hordes of ramblers.)

Continue up the tarmac road and you will begin to cross the well-tended park of Lowther Estate. After about 50m (54yd), a strange sight begins to materialize over the distant trees. A row of soaring turrets, a crenellated wall and Lowther Castle rise into view, like a gothic vision from a Disney cartoon.

Lowther Castle is a fake. It was built as a magnificent mansion between 1806 and 1811, commissioned by Sir John Lowther, the fifth Earl of Lonsdale (this being the hereditary title of the head of the Lowther family). The architect was Robert Smirke, who went on to design the British Museum. The Lowther Estate has been in the ownership of the Lowther family for more than 700 years, and there was a hall built here in the thirteenth century. The family lived in Lowther Castle until 1936, when death duties forced them to move out to the more modest accommodation of Askham Hall. The bulk of the building was pulled down, leaving only the impressive facade – a great pity the National Trust didn't get there first.

As you walk up the lane, notice how the oak trees form an avenue on either side. When you reach the T-junction at the top of the park, the avenue continues to march ahead, straight across the park towards the castle. Turn right at the junction and walk downhill towards the church.

🐦 *A church stood on this site in the twelfth century, but the present St Michael's is mostly Victorian. It is the family burial place of the Lowther family, and in 1857 they added the mausoleum in the churchyard. Sir John Lowther (the fifth Earl of Lonsdale; see page 76) sponsored the Lonsdale Belt in boxing. He was known as the Yellow Earl, not for any lack of bravery but because his favourite colour was yellow; he made all his servants wear the colour and passed it on to the Automobile Association when he became their first president.*

Once over the cattle grid by the church, turn immediately left and cross the stile into a field (signed 'Public footpath'). Bear right, diagonally across the field, towards another stile in the fence at the edge of the woods. Once into the woods, the path bears round to the left and continues in a nice level fashion, the ground rolling away to your right to the River Lowther. The river itself is out of view, but you may be able to spot Askham church again through the trees. The path is not tremendously well defined, but to begin with you will be running roughly parallel with the fence and walking through very pleasant mixed woodland, with one or two less common species such as maple. Look out for red squirrels.

After passing an old stretch of fence, the path begins a gentle descent. Notice the ornate iron bench which curves around the base of an oak on your right. Just past this, the path arrives at a T-junction. Turn left and the path will bring you to the old stone wall surrounding the castle gardens. At the wall, you will join a track and should head right. About 50m (54yd) further on the track forks and you should go right, descending through a very pretty wood with tantalizing glimpses of the river between the trees. Once you leave the woods via a farm gate, you will cross more carefully tended park land and get a brilliant view of the river below you. It is very wide and gentle, curving against the backdrop of the pine forest on the opposite shore, with the Lakeland fells visible in the distance.

The track heads along the riverbank through splendid parkland. The wall around the castle grounds runs along a limestone bluff on your left, high at the top of the field. Running your eye along, it is tricky to spot where the wall ends and the limestone begins. You can also just see the roof of a pagoda in the grounds, with what appears to be a tree growing through its shingle roof. As you walk beside the river, notice the water trough sunk into the hillside to conceal it from view from the castle. This is real parkland and it is

wonderful to see it in such good condition. There is a lovely sweep of hillside away to your left.

The track brings you to a fence line. Go through the farm gate and the path then splits. Go right, keeping to a permissive footpath rather than the right of way. The track follows the bend in the river and arrives at a narrow country lane. Once in the lane, go right, over Crookwath Bridge, and follow the lane back towards Askham. After walking for about 10 minutes, you will pass two public footpath signs on either side of the road. Go right, over a stone wall and into a small mixed plantation. At the next gate, cross the stile and go straight along the track, keeping the woods on your left and the fields on your right. You will now get a view back across the river and fields to the earlier path, and of the limestone escarpment.

When the plantation ends, keep on the track and where it swings left, go straight ahead over a stile (look out for the yellow marker arrow) and straight across the field, keeping the stone wall on your left. Follow the wall around to another farm gate. Go through this and you will be walking along the bottom of a field, with another wood on your right. There is a good view of Askham Hall ahead. Keep to the wire fence on your right and you will drop down to a track which emerges from the wood. Go left and pass into the graveyard via a small wooden gate. You now rejoin the river on your right. Still keeping to the line of the metal fence, the path skirts the graveyard and goes through another gate, into the churchyard proper.

There was a church on this site in the thirteenth century dedicated to St Columba. The present church is dedicated to St Peter and was rebuilt by Robert Smirke in 1832. Inside are memorials to the Sandford family. Robert Southey's son, Charles, was vicar here until his death in 1888.

You can go either way through the churchyard. If you go right you will get a view of the river, and when you emerge on the main road through the village, divert right for the view of Lowther River from Askham Bridge. After that, it's back up the hill to the centre of the village. Careful timing will ensure that the Punchbowl Inn is open.

Opposite: Askham church and bridge, seen from the woods south of Castlesteads

VISITOR ATTRACTIONS

Lowther Leisure Park
Hackthorpe, Penrith
Tel: 01931 712523
Extensive parkland with deer park, narrow-gauge railway and small circus.

Lakeland Bird of Prey Centre
Lowther Park, Hackthorpe, Penrith
Tel: 01931 712746
A breeding and training centre for falcons, with displays all year round.

15 TAYLORGILL FORCE & SPRINKLING TARN

Turn off the B5289 Borrowdale road at Seatoller Bridge (signed 'Seathwaite'). As you approach Seathwaite Farm, you can park on the wide grass verge (GR 235122). Parking is limited. There are two alternatives for the start of the walk

DISTANCE
9km (5½ miles); add an extra 1.4km (1 mile) if starting from Seathwaite Bridge

TERRAIN
This is the most strenuous walk in the book, involving a steep climb to Taylorgill Force along a path which is rough and unstable. Following the route in the direction described leaves the easier gradient for the descent, with more freedom to take in the view

This is an excellent – if strenuous – mountain walk from the heart of Borrowdale, the most rugged and dramatic of the Lakeland dales. A sharp climb takes you up to Taylorgill Force, for my money the most spectacular waterfall in Cumbria. From there it is an easy climb to Styhead Tarn and Sprinkling Tarn, in the midst of the mountains. Finally, you make a straightforward descent via Grains Gill with spectacular views of Borrowdale, Derwent Water and the northern fells.

Note: Use proper walking boots with ankle support and good grip. A good head for heights is useful.

STARTING POINT 1

If you are close to the farm, or have arrived by bus, follow the lane to Seathwaite Farm and go straight into the farmyard. Note that the farmhouse does teas if you are back in time. A few metres into the farmyard, there is an archway in the barn on your right. Go through it and follow the track between the fields to a footbridge. Cross over, and the footpath splits three ways. Go left through the wooden gate.

STARTING POINT 2

If you have arrived late and have been forced to park further from the farm, you can avoid the road altogether. Walk back over Seathwaite road bridge and then turn immediately left, through a small wooden gate (signed 'Public footpath'). Cross over the stile next to the farm gate and then follow the path along the riverbank. It heads upstream, winding through bracken and past a conifer plantation. As you walk the path, notice the heavily reinforced riverbank on the far side: this area has the highest measured rainfall in the Lake District. (In fact, Seathwaite has the dubious distinction of being the wettest inhabited place in Britain, with an annual rainfall of over 3m (120 in), and measurements have been taken here since Victorian times.) You will eventually arrive at a wooden farm gate. Go through it and walk along the bank to a wooden footbridge over Sourmilk Gill. The path splits three ways

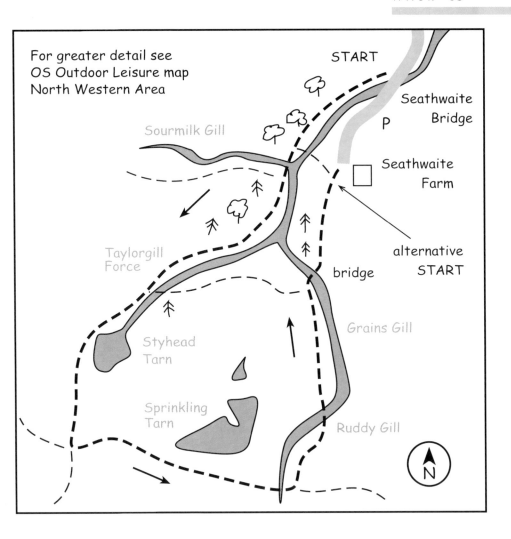

For greater detail see
OS Outdoor Leisure map
North Western Area

START

Seathwaite
Bridge

Sourmilk Gill

P

Seathwaite
Farm

Taylorgill
Force

bridge

alternative
START

Styhead
Tarn

Grains Gill

Sprinkling
Tarn

Ruddy Gill

N

here. The left-hand option crosses the footbridge to Seathwaite
Farm. Go straight on, through the small gate in the stone wall.

THE path sticks to the bank of the river. In summer the river is
reduced to a trickle, but come here after a winter thaw and it
is a major force of nature. Look up the fell to the right and you
may spot climbers practising on a distinctive outcrop of rock.

The path becomes rougher and goes past a conifer plantation.
Look out along here for butterwort, a fleshy green carnivorous
plant. The path climbs gradually to leave the conifers behind, winding up a fellside field. You will cross another wall via a ladder stile
and then begin to climb more steeply. You have now left the river
below but the path is still distinct, although boggy in places. You

will pass through another old wall, when you should turn back for a view of Blencathra and the motorway coming down from Watendlath.

The path crosses an outcrop of rock, and as you approach the gully you will begin to hear the rush of water. Within a dozen metres the view of Taylorgill Force is astonishing. The path now becomes very rough and winds steeply below a crag to what must be the Lake District's shortest stone wall. It juts out from the crag on your right, runs a few metres to the drop to the gully and then stops. Go through the gate and you will find yourself climbing along a precipitous path overlooking the gully, with a sheer drop to your left. Concentrate on the magnificent view of the waterfall ahead and it may keep your mind off the fact that a great deal of this path is permanently on the move.

The path drops to a stone wall and then climbs again. You are now following a wall and walking uphill, climbing level with the waterfall. This is a good opportunity to look back at the path you have just followed and the view down into the ravine. Where the stone wall becomes a wire fence there is a stile, and you can cross to a shady picnic spot in the trees, right at the head of Taylorgill Force.

♪ *Probably the Lake District's finest waterfall, Taylorgill Force plummets 42m (137 ft) down a cleft in the rocks to provide a spectacle known locally as the White Maid of Borrowdale. The waterfall marks the edge of a hanging valley created during the last Ice Age.*

Back on the path, continue climbing past the trees and into the head of an open, V-shaped valley. There is a dramatic view on the

Above: *The view of Great End from Sty Head Tarn*

Left: *Seathwaite Fell and Taylorgill Force seen from below Stockley Bridge*

left of Aaron Crag, with Glaramara further round. The severe cleft in Hind Side is cut by Red Beck. You may see walkers on the far side of the beck following the bridleway, a packhorse route between Borrowdale and Wasdale.

As you approach the top of the valley, the stream forms cascades and one or two attractive pools. The path forks, the left-hand route crossing the river to descend the bridleway to Stockley Bridge and Seathwaite. Continue straight on, ignoring the wooden footbridge, and past a large cairn in the middle of an old stream bed, over a couple more becks and eventually to Styhead Tarn. This is a very pretty little tarn, overlooked by the massive grey bulk of Great End. On the right is Lingmell, then Scafell Pike, Broad End and back to Great End. A popular camping spot, this is an ideal place from which to launch yourself up a range of major Lakeland mountains.

Continue past Styhead Tarn, along a made path and up to the crest of the ridge. You will immediately encounter a large wooden box, which is the mountain rescue post at Sty Head. To save you the bother of looking in it, this contains first aid gear and a metal sled used to convey injured walkers and climbers rapidly down the fell.

This is a major crossroads of mountain routes. (There was once a proposal to take a road through here, linking Borrowdale with the west coast of Cumbria. The idea was last rejected by Cumberland County Council in 1934.) From here you could climb Scafell Pike, England's highest mountain, and then drop to Wasdale and Wast Water, the deepest of the 16 lakes. Or, you can go left and head to Sprinkling Tarn. Keep your eyes peeled and, if conditions are good, 200m (220yd) from the rescue box you will catch a glimpse of the Irish Sea.

After 10 minutes you will have climbed from Sty Head to walk alongside a small beck, which splashes down a narrow gully lined with parsley fern. The path crosses the beck, there is another short climb and then you will suddenly find yourself at Sprinkling Tarn. This beats even Seathwaite for rainfall: over 5m (200in) a year has been recorded here. The tarn's Old English name was Prentibountern, meaning 'sparkling stream', and for a time it was known as Sparkling Tarn. This is a wild, isolated tarn, surrounded by mountain peaks. To the south are Great End and the Scafell range, to the west Lingmell and Great Gable.

Continue past the tarn and over the ridge, and you will drop to the head of Ruddy Gill (so named because of the high iron content of the soil). The path which goes over the gill and straight ahead would take you to Angle Tarn and down into Langdale valley – a bit inconvenient if you have parked at Seathwaite. Instead, cross the gill – which is an eroded gully just here – and turn left down the narrow ravine on your left. A superb view opens up and as you descend you can see Blencathra in the distance, then a tremendous prospect of Skiddaw and Derwent Water, with Castle Crag in the middle distance.

The ravine is a dark cleft in the rocks and is covered with a variety of mosses, lichens and ferns, despite the efforts of ill-educated gill scramblers. It is a long walk down, but this is made easier by the well-constructed path and the wonderful view. You will cross Ruddy Gill via a wooden footbridge and then Grains Gill comes in from the right. Ignore the next footbridge and continue down to a wooden gate in a stone wall. Once through, follow the wall downhill until you reach a gate and stone bridge. Go right, through the gate and over Stockley Bridge.

🔊 *A sturdy, traditionally built structure, this bridge stands on the packhorse route between Borrowdale and Wasdale. (This is not the original bridge, which was severely damaged in storms in August 1966, when 130mm (5in) of rain fell in an hour.) Just below the bridge is an excellent pool, popular with bathers after the long descent from Scafell Pike.*

As you continue downhill, you will catch a glimpse of Taylorgill Force again. The path drops to a stile over a wire fence and continues downstream. Notice the long wall running along the fell on the far side, which prevents adventurous local sheep escaping to Ennerdale.

The path drops to the right of an odd, narrow conifer plantation and you will lose sight of the river again. Continue straight on between the field boundaries, through two more farm gates and finally into the yard at Seathwaite Farm. The right of way goes left, past the farmhouse and sheep pens. (If you have arrived here late, note that there is a telephone box on the right.) You can either go left, through the archway and back along the river to Seathwaite Bridge, or straight through the farmyard to the road.

VISITOR ATTRACTIONS
See Walk 10: River Greta.

Overleaf:
*Fleetwith Pike
reflected at dawn
in the freezing
water of
Buttermere*

THE LAKES

16 CONISTON WATER

PARKING AND START/FINISH
The walk starts from the car park at Torver, Beckstones, opposite the Lakeland Land Rover garage (GR 286933), 1km (⅔ mile) south of Torver on the A5084 to Lowick. There is additional parking at the halfway point of the walk, about 500m (⅓ mile) south of Beckstones at GR 287927

DISTANCE
6km (3¾ miles)

TERRAIN
The first part of the walk (along the shore) is relatively easy; the second, up to Torver Tarn, is harder, involving a moderate climb. As the circuit is almost a figure-of-eight, it is possible to treat it as two separate walks, linked by a short stretch of road

The south-west corner of Coniston, around Blawith and Torver, has a character distinct from anywhere else in the Lakes. Bracken-covered common, rushing becks lined with juniper, and above it all the magnificent presence of the Old Man of Coniston. It is also wonderfully secluded, and although the road sometimes gets busy you only have to walk a few hundred metres on to the common and you are in a world of your own. This route covers one of the best walks on Torver Common, combining it with a walk along Coniston's wonderful shoreline.

Facing the car park with your back towards the Land Rover garage, the path leaves via the top left-hand corner. A track leads up to a farm gate and kissing gate, and once through you will be on Torver Common and National Park Authority access land. There is a beck immediately in front of you; don't cross, but go left and follow the less distinct track by the stone wall. This brings you to the first of the three tarns on this walk – Kelly Hall Tarn, a small, reedy affair in a shallow bowl in the moor.

Continue left past the corner of the wall and you will come to a good view of the Old Man of Coniston, with the craggy ridge of Dow Crag running into it from the left. The path works around a rocky knoll, keeping to a second stone wall and fence on your left. When you reach the corner of the wall, the path splits. The Ordnance Survey would have you go left, but this route can be boggy and difficult to follow. Besides, that way you would miss one of the best views in the area. So go straight on, following the distinct narrow path along the edge of the hill on your right.

You will now be walking towards what at first appears to be a somewhat pathetic, boggy pond but as you approach, your high viewpoint will reveal it to be a long, narrow tarn known as Long Moss. Keep going and the view will suddenly open out: by the time you reach the end of the hill, level with the foot of Long Moss, you will have a superb panorama which takes in Coniston Water, the Old Man and, beyond, Fairfield and the central Lakeland fells. The view to the left is particularly fine, as the road is concealed in the valley and there is little sign of human habitation, just rolling,

88

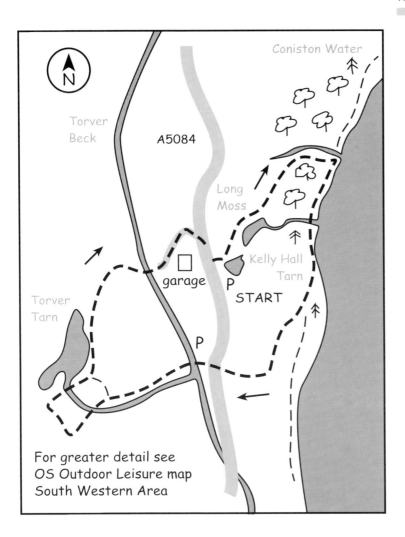

Coniston Water

Torver
Beck

A5084

Long
Moss

garage

P

Kelly Hall
Tarn

START

Torver
Tarn

P

For greater detail see
OS Outdoor Leisure map
South Western Area

bracken-covered moor leading your eye to the distinctive peak of
the Old Man. Looking along the moor there is a sharp pinnacle
above the bracken, overlooking the lake. The green path to the left
is your route.

Follow the path down the hill, past the end of Long Moss and
across the moor, walking roughly parallel to Coniston Water. The
route is a little indistinct at times, as it makes its way down through
a little valley and then up to the pinnacle, passing a holly tree on
the left. Walk past the famous pinnacle (an outcrop of rock well
worth climbing for another fabulous view) and head straight
towards the distant mountains. The path begins to drop downhill
and you will be able to see the head of Coniston Water, Brantwood
in the distance on the far shore, and the Coniston Boating Centre
just visible in the north-west corner of the lake.

✿ *Coniston Water is one of four lakes designated a public highway. The ore from Coppermines Valley used to be transported down the lake and loaded aboard ships at Greenodd, when that village was a thriving port (before the estuary silted up). Its status as a highway has never been rescinded, which means that powered craft are permitted to use it, although (fortunately, in my opinion), speed restrictions now deter power boats from blasting along its length. The lake was originally known as Thorstein's Water, after one of Lakeland's many Norse settlers. It is 8km (5miles) long, 0.8km (½ mile) wide and 55m (175ft) at its deepest point.*

Coniston Water was the scene of Donald Campbell's ill-fated world water-speed record attempt in 1967. In his boat Bluebird he had already set a record of 202.32mph on Ullswater in 1955, then 276.3mph on Lake Dumbleyung in Australia in 1964, and raised it to over 280mph on Coniston Water in 1966. During his final attempt, on 4 January 1967, the official timekeepers recorded a speed of 318mph before Bluebird – only 43m (140ft) from the final marker – soared into the air, somersaulted and vanished into the water. Campbell's body was, sadly, never recovered. There is a slate memorial to him in Coniston village.

A view of the snow-capped Old Man of Coniston from Torver Tarn

After 40m (43yd) or so, another path comes in from the left. Go right, parallel to a stone wall and a powerful beck, and you will be walking through a veritable forest of juniper. Keep to the right-hand bank of the stream and it will lead you down to a wire fence and a farm gate. Once through, you will find yourself in a pleasant coppiced woodland, planted on the steeply sloping side of Torver Common. The path peels off from the beck and follows a stone wall, which stands between you and a pretty larch wood.

The path drops to the lakeshore. Turn right to follow a delight-ful lakeside path. Although you will have your back to the fells along here, there are good views to the foot of the lake. Look out for sailing dinghies and the magnificent National Trust *Gondola*.

♫ The Gondola *is unequivocally the nicest form of powered transport in the Lake District (I might be tempted to extend that to the whole country). Launched in 1860 as a passenger craft and run by the Furness Railway Company, this 25.8m (84ft) long craft was built in Liverpool at a cost of £1000 and transported to Coniston Water in sections.* Gondola *continued as a passenger boat until 1936, after which it was used for a while as a houseboat, before being wrecked by a storm in the 1960s. The National Trust rescued the craft from the scrap heap, only to sink it again to preserve the iron hull until funds were available to restore it. After a magnificent research and restoration job, the refitted* Gondola *was launched in 1980.*

The path passes a number of small bays and pebble beaches. There is no evidence of a road on the far shore, but you may hear the occasional car and sometimes, on a still day, the voices of picnick-ers. This is an idyllic little path and is rapidly becoming one of my favourite lakeshore footpaths. The route is level, easy to follow and there is nothing to distract you from admiring the views over the water.

You will leave the wood behind as the path continues along the shore, with open common above you to the right. This means that the views get even better, although this is only for a short while as you then plunge into a copse of trees. After half-an-hour or so of steady walking, you will pass a small bench seat. This is a brilliant place for picnics and a good vantage point for *Gondola* spotting, as it is directly opposite the pier at Parkamoor. Look a little to the right and you will be able to make out Peel Island.

♫ The area around Torver and the southern end of Coniston Water *should be familiar to all Arthur Ransome fans. His famous children's book* Swallows and Amazons *was based around here, although Ransome changed most of the names. The basic geography, however, stayed the same, and in her excellent book* Arthur Ransome and Captain Flint's Trunk *Christina Hardyment tracked down most of the original locations. Peel Island is the site of the Secret Harbour and Wild Cat Island, the River Crake is the Amazon, Allan Tarn is Octopus*

*Lagoon and the Old Man is Kanchenjunga. Further afield, Bowness
became Rio and Belle Isle was Long Island.*

*Ransome went to school in Windermere and lived for part of his
exceptionally adventurous adult life near Coniston. He died in 1967
and is buried in Rusland churchyard. At the Museum of Lakeland Life
and Industry in Kendal there is a re-creation of his study, featuring
Ransome's original desk.*

About 100m (110yd) beyond the bench the path leaves the shore
and climbs the hill, just as you reach a stone wall. Notice the stone
boathouse on the far side. The path levels out and runs alongside
the wall for a short distance, passing a silver birch which clings
precariously to the top of a rock outcrop, right by the path. About
100m (110yd) past the silver birch, the path becomes over-excited
and fans out in all directions. Unless you double back on yourself,
it doesn't really matter which route you take. The easiest is to stay
with the wall for a little longer, after which the path bends to the
right past a small pond and climbs alongside a wire fence to a farm
gate and kissing gate. Go through and follow the path right, across
the common. You will be nearing the road again, so take care if you
have children and/or dogs with you. The path begins to drop and
you can now look across the valley to the river and a footpath on
the far side of the road. In a few minutes you will be climbing the
steep hill in front of you, unless you opt for the short option (see
below).

The path drops to the road beside a small car-parking space. If
you are running out of time or members of the party are beginning
to flag, you can curtail the walk at this point by turning right and
following the road for 500m (⅓ mile) back to the Land Rover
garage. You can always come back and do the second half of the
walk another day.

If you want to complete the walk, go straight across the road to
a kissing gate (signed 'Public footpath') and another National Park
Authority sign for Torver Common. The path drops down through
a gorse-covered field and after 60m (65yd) you will arrive at Torver
Beck. This is a fast-flowing river and it is sometimes possible to
cross via stepping stones. However, the National Park Authority has
installed an excellent footbridge just 20m (22yd) upstream. As you
cross the beck to the alder-lined far bank, you should look out for
dippers.

Once over the stile at the end of the footbridge, the path splits
three ways. Go straight, up the open fellside, following Mere Beck
upstream. This beck is lined with juniper – in fact, this must have
once been a juniper wood, now long since cleared by charcoal
burners. Note the electricity poles: this is one of the few areas of
the Lake District where the ground is so rocky that it has been
impossible to run the cables underground. The bright yellow

Looking south over Coniston Water from a vantage point near Long Moss Tarn

'Danger of death' stickers on each pole don't do a great deal to enhance the landscape.

Follow the line of the poles uphill, passing a small landslip on the left. Look out for the wild rose bush just as you cross a small beck. Immediately after a small peat bog the path moves away from the river and forks. The right-hand option is a narrow, eroded path. Go left and a wide path will bring you to another beck and a little cascade. Cross over the beck and walk up the hill, and after another 70m (76yd) the path will swing right to join the narrow eroded path you have just spurned. Go left up a slight rise and you will have a surprise view of the tarn in the foreground, with the magnificent spectacle of the Old Man of Coniston and Wetherlam in the distance.

The path takes you below the electricity cables again and down to the shore of Torver Tarn, next to the old reservoir wall. This tarn lies in open moorland (the result of extensive deforestation in the sixteenth century to provide fuel for the local iron bloomeries). Despite the low wall, it is a natural tarn, the damming having been done to increase the water supply to a nearby bobbin mill. It can be a wild spot, the wind whipping across the moor and humming in the overhead wires, but on a sunny summer's day it is glorious to stroll along beside the water with the dramatic peaks in the distance.

The path swings up on to the hill on the right, continuing parallel to the tarn. Ahead you will now see the houses of Torver village and another cracking view of the Old Man, with Holme Fell and Loughrigg in the distance. Next, the path takes you down the hill past the end of the tarn and towards two converging stone walls. The view is somewhat spoilt by the messy Land Rover garage (I wish they would plant a few trees to screen it). The path will bring you to a farm gate where the walls almost meet. Go down the narrow track, which takes you alongside the fields, past a bank barn and on to a narrow lane beside Mill Bridge.

The neat white house opposite is built on the site of an old mill (look for the mill stone beside the gate). The route goes across the bridge, but first it is worth going up the bridlepath to the left of the house, through the gate and into the wood. Look down through the trees and you will be able to see the feeder stream and sluice gate for the waterwheel. Go back, and cross the bridge. There is a pleasant, tranquil mill pond on your right as you cross, surrounded by trees. Turn left on the other side of the bridge, and as you pass through the farm gate look back into the trees and you will see the remains of the mill building and overshot waterwheel.

Continue up the track to the main road. Turn right, past Emlin Hall, and the road will then bring you back to the car park and starting point.

VISITOR ATTRACTIONS

Coniston Launches
Castle Buildings, Near Sawrey, Ambleside
Tel: 015394 36216
A regular launch service on the lake.

Gondola Steam Launch
Coniston
Tel: 015394 41288
The best way to see the lake, travelling in Victorian splendour. Note that sailings are restricted to good weather. To check that the *Gondola* is running, telephone the Coniston tourist information centre (see Appendix 3).

Coniston Boating Centre
Lake Road, Coniston
Tel: 015394 41366
Run by the National Park Authority, the centre offers launching facilities and boat storage. It also hires out dinghies, rowing boats, canoes and environmentally friendly electric-powered motor boats. There is a good café on site.

For other Coniston attractions, see Walk 13: Levers Water & Church Beck.

17 BUTTERMERE

PARKING AND START/FINISH
The walk starts from the National Park Authority pay-and-display car park behind the Bridge Hotel. Be warned: this gets full very early in summer. There is an additional lay-by on the road to Newlands Valley, but please don't park on the grass verges

DISTANCE
6.4km (4 miles)

TERRAIN
Mostly level walking, with a short, steep climb above the tunnel section

This is a classic circuit of the prettiest of the smaller lakes. It is possible to keep to the lakeshore for most of the route, with an ever-changing perspective of the surrounding mountains. This is an ideal walk for families and anyone wanting a rest from the high fells.

FROM the car park, walk past the Bridge Hotel back to the main road and turn right towards Wilkinsyke Farm. Follow the track into the farmyard (signed 'Public bridleway, lakeshore path'), between the houses and out via the stile by the farm gate (signed 'Footpath'). Once past the farm you will have a good view of Buttermere, High Stile – the fell above the far shore – and Sourmilk Gill, the waterfall in the trees. This is a good way to avoid the queues, as most walkers tend to take the anti-clockwise route around the lake.

The path takes you through a field to another farm gate. Go right, following the sign for the lakeshore path, and you will find yourself walking down a recently made permissive path between the field boundaries. At the bottom, go through another gate and down a short flight of stone steps. The path takes you around the edge of a field to a kissing gate and the entrance to Pike Rigg woods. Go through another kissing gate and you will be on the lakeshore.

The name Buttermere is usually interpreted as 'the lake by the dairy pastures', although there is an older derivation from Buthar, the Norse owner of the lake. It is 2km (1¼ miles) long, less than 28m (91ft) deep and is home to the char, a comparatively rare Lakeland fish. The lake is owned by the National Trust. Buttermere and Crummock Water were once one large lake, formed by the last Ice Age. Debris that was washed into the valley formed the delta which now separates them.

Buttermere was a well-known beauty spot in Wordsworth's day and was once the scene of a national scandal. In 1792, Captain Joseph Budworth published a guidebook to the area, A Fortnight's Ramble in the Lakes. He went into raptures over the innocent beauty of one Mary Robinson, the inn keeper's 15-year-old daughter at the

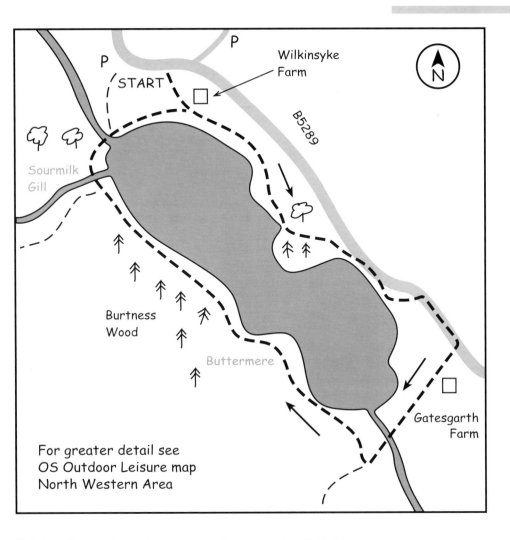

P

P

START

Wilkinsyke
Farm

B5289

Sourmilk
Gill

Burtness
Wood

Buttermere

Gatesgarth
Farm

For greater detail see
OS Outdoor Leisure map
North Western Area

*Fish Inn. He sang her praises at such embarrassing length that he
toned down his remarks in subsequent editions for fear of attracting
unsavoury characters.*

*In 1802, the Honourable Alexander Augustus Hope, MP for
Linlithgow, arrived in the area, was a big hit with the locals, and
within six weeks had married Mary Robinson at Lorton church.
Samuel Taylor Coleridge was living at Keswick at the time and was
a correspondent for the London* Morning Post. *He duly wrote up the
romantic courtship, emphasizing what a lucky catch the inn keeper's
daughter had made. It began to look less lucky, however, when
Charles Hope reported that his brother was at the time enjoying a
holiday in Europe. The bogus MP was revealed to be James Hatfield,
a noted swindler and bigamist. There was an immense outcry, not
least among the local gentry who had been so keen to suck up
to him.*

As soon as Hatfield and his new wife arrived back from their honeymoon in Scotland, he was arrested. He used his talents to persuade the local constabulary to allow him to go fishing for the day and, not surprisingly, didn't come back. He escaped over the fells to Ravenglass (which was a major port at the time) and caught a ship to Liverpool, but was arrested several weeks later in Wales, tried in Carlisle and hanged – not for bigamy, but for defrauding the post office by franking his letters as an MP. The severity of the sentence was in part due to the national sympathy for Mary, which had been whipped up by the press. Mary remarried in 1808 and died in 1837. She is buried in Caldbeck churchyard.

The story was immediately taken up by writers and playwrights. Wordsworth praised Mary's virtue in his epic poem The Prelude. *The latest contribution to the genre is Melvyn Bragg's* The Maid of Buttermere, *published in 1987. The George Shelbourn who appears in Mr Bragg's novel is a distant relation of mine.*

The trees restrict your view of the lake to begin with, but this quickly turns into a lovely easy walk along the wooded lakeshore. Shortly after the third kissing gate, look out for the view of Hay Stacks and Warnscale Beck at the far end of the lake. Hay Stacks is an excellent walk and was the favourite of the pioneer fell walker

Rowing boats on Buttermere, 'the lake by the dairy pastures'

99

and guidebook writer, Alfred Wainwright. After his death in 1991, his ashes were scattered on the mountain. There is a memorial to him in Buttermere church.

The route now becomes like a garden path, being level and easy to follow. After kissing gate number four, the route makes its way through parkland and past a group of lime trees. This is a good route for tree spotting – look out for sycamore, oak, lime and the occasional sweet chestnut. As you approach the next kissing gate, there is a park bench between two lime trees which makes a good spot for a picnic or simply to sit and take in the view.

The footpath used to go through a rock tunnel at this point, but the roof became unstable and the tunnel has been closed. This is a pity, as it was a great hit with children of all ages. (George Benson, the nineteenth-century owner of nearby Hassness House, built the tunnel so that he would have an unimpeded route around the lake – it also kept his workforce occupied in winter.) The route now climbs steeply over the tunnel, starting at the rock outcrop just to the left of the tunnel entrance. The first part of the climb is a scramble, but once you are at the top it becomes a delightful walk through woodland again. Look out for a spectacular outcrop of rock in the trees above you on your left, as you start to descend.

Once back on the lakeshore path, go through another kissing gate and walk on to a tree-lined shingle beach. The lake will eventually be full of flat stones skipped across the water at this point – the temptation is tremendous. Leaving the trees behind, follow the path through another kissing gate and past a small plantation of firs. There is a dramatic view of Fleetwith Pike ahead and on the opposite shore you can see Comb Beck tumbling down from High Crag. When you pass a sign for 'Permissive lakeshore path', bear right and keep to the shore. After another kissing gate, the path runs just below the main road, so take care with children and dogs at this point. Another 300m (325yd) and the path joins the road, beside another beach.

The next 600m (650yd) are along the road. Keep close to the walls and watch out for traffic. After a few minutes' walking you will come to the road bridge over Gatesgarth Beck. Once over it, turn right, along the permissive path by Gatesgarth Farm. (The car park opposite the farm is more expensive than the one at Buttermere village, but does offer a useful alternative starting point if Buttermere is full. It also has the advantage of a permanently stationed ice-cream van in the school holidays.)

The path works its way around the farm to a cluster of gates. Go through the small gate signed 'Lake shore path' and follow the path across the fields. You will get an amazing view to your left of Fleetwith Pike, Hay Stacks and Warnscale Beck. This part of the valley is a popular starting point for the climb to Great Gable and Scafell Pike. Once through the gate on the far side of the fields, the path forks. Unless you have an overriding urge to include Ennerdale on the itinerary, turn right (signed 'Public bridleway: Buttermere').

You will cross a beck as it dashes through the rocks and then leave the bridleway to go right, along the permissive lakeshore path. After about 10 minutes' walking, you will enter Burtness Wood. Like most of this area, the wood is owned and managed by the National Trust. A short distance into the woods the path forks. Go right and keep to the shore for a view of the woods at Hassness, on the far shore. Once again, there are a few conveniently placed benches along the way.

The path rejoins the main track and plunges through an intriguing swathe of beech trees, which seem out of place among all the fir. Walk through the woods towards the foot of the lake, arriving eventually at a fence and a pair of gates. The path left climbs to Red Pike and Ennerdale. Keep right, going through the wooden gate and across a pair of wooden bridges, which take you over Sourmilk Gill and Buttermere Dubs. Again, there is an excellent view of Fleetwith at the head of the lake.

Once over the second bridge, you will have a choice. If you head straight on, you will leave the field to join a farm lane which eventually takes you back to the Bridge Hotel and the centre of the village. This is the way most people come out from the village. In recent years, a more attractive alternative has been negotiated which goes along the edge of the lake and across the fields. This is the route you now take, but bear in mind that it is closed during lambing time.

Turn right from the bridge and put all dogs on leads immediately, as you may encounter livestock. Following the shore means you get the benefit of the terrific view of the mountains at the far end of the lake. Amateur photographers take note that there are plenty of overhanging branches along here to frame that prizewinning photograph.

The path crosses five fields, keeping to the shore throughout. Each field boundary has a stile and there are one or two with wire flaps for dogs. Finally, you will leave the fifth field and cross a small beck, and the path then goes left, up the field to join the outward path. Make your way back into the village for tea and scones at one of the hotels.

VISITOR ATTRACTIONS
For the nearest attractions, see Walk 10: River Greta.

18 LOWESWATER

PARKING AND START/FINISH
The walk starts from the National Trust pay-and-display car park at Maggie's Bridge (GR 135210). To find this, head north west along the minor road between Loweswater village and Mockerkin and turn left just after the old Loweswater school (signed 'Public bridleway'). The turning is 100m (110yd) beyond the turning right to Thackthwaite. Alternative parking is available along the road beside Loweswater or at the National Trust Lanthwaite Wood car park

DISTANCE
6.5km (4 miles)

TERRAIN
Very easy walking for the most part with a short, steep climb up the lane at Miresyke

Located in the north-west corner of the Lake District National Park, Loweswater is an excellent place to head for when the central lakes have become too busy. It lies in splendid seclusion, out beyond the further reaches of Crummock Water and Buttermere. The valley is peaceful and rural and the lake tends to be appreciated more by locals than visitors. This is a superb walk along a tree-lined shore, with a short climb to the added bonus of a view to the Solway Firth and Scotland.

EAVING the car park, continue down the lane and through the gate (signed 'Watergate Farm, Watergate Cottage and Holme Wood Bothy'). Cross over Dub Beck and follow the track through pleasant, open farmland.

When you reach the first cattle grid, ignore the stile on the right which tempts you to the foot of the lake. Continue along the track and enjoy the view of Darling Fell on the far side of the lake. The track leads you across fields and then approaches a group of houses (Holme Wood and Watergate House). About 50m (54yd) from the house the path goes right, across the field, to a stile and farm gate at the entrance to Holme Wood. Cross over the stile and

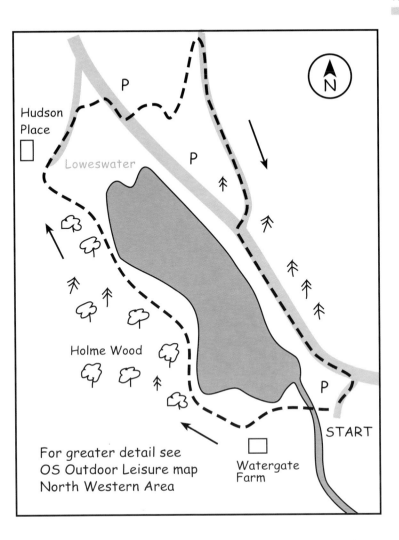

Hudson
Place

Loweswater

P

P

N

Holme Wood

For greater detail see
OS Outdoor Leisure map
North Western Area

Watergate
Farm

START

you will find a park bench on your right, which is useful if you fancy a stop to take in the view of Loweswater.

♪ Loweswater means 'the leafy lake', derived from the Old Norse name Laufs-saer-vatn. *It is owned by the National Trust and is only 2.4km (1½ miles) long by 0.8km (½ mile) wide. At its deepest point it is 18.2m (60ft) and it is unique among the 16 lakes in that water leaving it flows towards the centre of the Lake District.*

You are now on a lovely wooded track, with reeds and lapping water by your side as you follow the path through the trees. It is very peaceful. At various points you will have good views of Loweswater Fell and Whiteside. From the deciduous woodland, you will then enter an area predominantly of conifers. After a few metres you will cross a small beck (via two wooden railway

Opposite: A ford across the stream through picturesque Holme Wood

103

sleepers), and the path then forks. The main track goes straight ahead, but instead you should follow the path to the right in order to keep to the lakeshore. You will come to a stone hut in the woods, beside the lake. This is Holme Wood Bothy, owned by the National Trust, and is a wonderful place to camp.

Continue along the path, keeping to the lakeshore whenever it forks. You will eventually come to a fence. Follow the path left to rejoin the forestry track, then turn right to a farm gate and stile. Cross into the field and continue along the path. This is a reedy lakeside field, so look out for pied flycatcher, grebe and, in winter, goldeneye. The view is very pretty, particularly back along the lake, with little sign of human cultivation.

You will reach another gate, which takes you on to a narrow track between two stone walls and, after a couple of minutes' walking, to Hudson Place, an eighteenth-century farmhouse. Turn right and follow the tarmac lane downhill. Once past the farmhouse, ignore the path indicated to the left and continue down the lane (signed 'Waterend'). As the lane levels off, look out for a stile in the wire fence on your right (next to the metal farm gate). Cross the stile and walk straight across the field towards a stile in the fence on the far side. You will cross a wooden causeway over the marsh. Climb over the stile (note the dog stile next to it), cross a small beck and then bear right to another stile in the hedge on your right. Once over, the path goes left up the field, to arrive at a kissing gate and the main road.

Turn right, and you could follow the road back to the track which leads to the National Trust car park. However, it is nearly 2km (1¼ miles) and a bit tedious, so there is an alternative route. Just past the telephone box, there is a lane on the left (signed 'Public bridleway to Mossergate'). Go up this steep, narrow lane (look out for a farm gate and good views) until it peters out into a rough track at a T-junction.

Turn left, then immediately right, up another rough lane (signed 'Path to Mosserfell'). This section is steep and rough underfoot. It takes you up to a farm gate and, once through, you will find yourself in a fellside field with increasingly good views back over the lake. When you get to the next farm gate, that distant hazy patch you may be able to see ahead of you is the sea at the Solway Firth and, beyond it, Scotland. Go through the gate and walk on uphill to the next one. Climb over the stile and turn sharp right, heading back in the direction of Loweswater. Once around a corner, there are lovely views of the lake.

As you can tell from the grass growing down the centre, this tarmac lane is not heavily used. Ignore the footpath left to Foulsyke and continue down the lane, into a small wood, and on to the main road again. Turn left along the road (and look out for the neat weather vane on Crabtree Beck House). Despite the proximity of the lake, there is no real lakeshore footpath along here. Continue along the road, and after about 1.5km (1 mile) you will arrive at the lane (signed 'Public bridleway') to the National Trust car park. (If you reach the school house, you've walked too far.) Turn right, down the lane and back to the car park.

VISITOR ATTRACTIONS

Loweswater village is not exactly packed with attractions, but Cockermouth is only a few kilometres to the north and offers the following:

Wordsworth House
Main Street, Cockermouth
Tel: 01900 824805
The birthplace of William and Dorothy Wordsworth. A fine Georgian mansion with a splendid garden, owned by the National Trust.

The Printing Museum
102 Main Street, Cockermouth
Tel: 01900 824984
A small, privately run collection of old printing blocks and machines, tucked around the back of Winkworth's secondhand bookshop.

Toy and Model Museum
Bank's Court, Market Place, Cockermouth
Tel: 01900 827606
An award-winning museum, exhibiting a wide range of toys from 1900 to the present, including a visitor-operated tinplate model railway.

Lakeland Sheep & Wool Centre
Egremont Road, Cockermouth
Tel: 01900 822673
Visitor centre devoted to the Lake District's major inhabitant. It includes a live sheep show.

Holme Wood Bothay
Contact National Trust Enterprises
Tel: 015394 35599
For the ultimate in picturesque accommodation.

19 THIRLMERE & HARROP TARN

PARKING AND START/FINISH
The walk starts from the North West Water car park at Steel End (GR 321129), at the south-west corner of the lake. Alternatively, to do the shorter route park at Dobgill car park (GR 316139), 1.2km (¾ mile) further along the road

DISTANCE
6.5km (4 miles) for the extended walk, 3.75km (2⅓ miles) if starting and finishing at Dobgill car park

TERRAIN
The route along the lakeshore is level, easy walking. The climb alongside Dob Gill is steep, although fairly secure underfoot. The descent is long and gentle

Until the early 1980s, access to Thirlmere shore was severely restricted. A reservoir for over 100 years, the Victorian filtration plant couldn't cope with hordes of grubby tourists splashing about in the water. After considerable improvement works and negotiation with the Lake District National Park Authority, the lake was opened to the public for the first time. There is now a permissive footpath along the entire western shore. The water is very clear and pure and the comparative lack of traffic makes this a delightful and attractive area to explore. This route combines a walk along the shore with a climb to a lovely secluded tarn in the trees above Birk Crag.

THERE are two starting points for this walk. Beginning at Steel End car park and walking along the shore to Dob Gill gives you a chance to warm up and enjoy the views before the stiff climb to Harrop Tarn. However, you have to retrace this 1.35km (⅘ mile) section at the end of the walk, so the alternative is to begin at the Dobgill car park. This has the benefit of a toilet block, so you might consider it a more civilized point at which to end the walk.

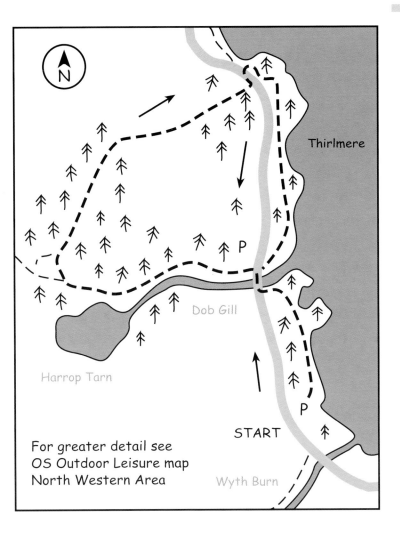

Thirlmere

P

Dob Gill

Harrop Tarn

For greater detail see
OS Outdoor Leisure map
North Western Area

START

P

Wyth Burn

FROM STEEL END CAR PARK

Leave the car park via the kissing gate and you will immediately
find yourself on a forestry path which winds through the trees,
alongside Wyth Burn (a curiously Scottish-sounding name for a
Lakeland beck). After 50m (54yd) or so you will leave the woods
and have a truly magnificent view of the western flanks of
Helvellyn, with the white streak of Whelpside Gill directly in front
of you.

The path is very clear and winds across open grass and marsh,
crossing a number of smaller becks before heading into the trees
again. Keeping to the edge of the forest, you will be able to see
Wythburn church on the far side of the valley, directly next to the
road. The path bends back into the woods, crossing three board-
walks before bringing you to the shore of Thirlmere.

*Opposite: The
impressive cas-
cade of Dob Gill
drops down
through rocks
and trees into the
pool below*

107

🔊 *In the 1870s, Manchester Corporation Water Works began campaigning to buy two small lakes, Leathes Water and Brackmere, in order to dam them and provide a new reservoir for Manchester. There was tremendous local and national opposition, objectors fearing that the beauty of the area would be ruined forever. A Thirlmere Defence Association was formed, questions were asked in Parliament and the local landowner – Thomas Leathe of Dalehead Hall – was so adamant that he would never sell the land that surveys had to be conducted by the Corporation in secret. But when Leathe died, his son sold the required 11,000 acres; the Thirlmere Bill was passed in 1879 and work began in 1886.*

The 30m (98ft) high dam raised the water level by 16.5m (54ft), flooding two small villages and creating the lake we see today. The first water arrived in Manchester in October 1894, carried there by a 153km (95 mile) gravity-fed aqueduct. A marvel of Victorian engineering, the aqueduct is over 2m (6½ft) in diameter and tunnels 460m (1500ft) through Dunmail Raise, which alone took four years to dig.

Interestingly, one of the chief objectors to the creation of Thirlmere was John Ruskin, who lived at Coniston at the time. The public outcry against the scheme helped establish the climate which gave birth to the National Trust, one year after the aqueduct was opened.

The name Thirlmere actually means 'a narrow stretch of water'. The lake is 5.6km (3½ miles) long, 0.8km (½ mile) wide and 48m (156ft) deep.

You will pass a marker post and then about 30m (33yd) beyond that the path winds to the edge of the wood to give you a clear view along the length of the lake to the easily recognizable shape of Blencathra. The shape gives the mountain its other, more prosaic name of Saddleback. Ignore the erosion path into the trees and keep to the edge of the wood, crossing rocks and stones for 60m (65yd) or so before coming to a wire fence. Walk through the gate and on to a rock outcrop for another good view of the lake.

The path now goes back into the woods, over a 30m (33yd) boardwalk and then begins to get boggy. The route follows the line of the overhead telegraph wires, bringing you alongside a wire fence. Follow the fence line to a forestry track and turn right, towards the lake. The track disappears very quickly and the path swings off left along the fence and the remains of a drystone wall. When you reach a marker post at a gap between two walls, turn left and head up the hill to the gate in the stone wall. (Alternatively, divert to the right for a look at Dob Gill.)

The gate will bring you out on to the road at Dobgill Bridge. Follow the road north, and 100m (110yd) beyond the bridge cross over into Dobgill car park. It is a common but confusing Lakeland habit to contract a name like Dob Gill into one word when another word like 'bridge', 'car park' or 'force' is added.)

FROM DOBGILL CAR PARK

At the top left-hand corner of the car park is a short flight of wooden steps which leads you up into the trees and is signed 'Harrop Tarn'. Climbing uphill, you encounter what must be the tallest kissing gate in the Lake District. This is designed to keep red deer away from the road. (When I walked this route one November, there was a sign on the gate which warned: 'Do not wander from the path, stalking in progress'. Climbing uphill through an early winter snowfall, this lent the forest an added air of danger and excitement. I didn't see anyone – apart from a couple of fell walkers also nervously peering through the trees – so perhaps it was a ruse to prevent ramblers crashing about through the woods.) Go through the kissing gate and up a stone path to begin climbing steeply through the trees. The path zigzags below an impressive rocky knoll, then winds around the side of the knoll to reach Dob Gill and an impressive cascade and pool.

Continue past the waterfall into the dark conifer forest. After a few minutes of gentle uphill walking, you will be in sight of Harrop Tarn. The tarn is only around 4.5m (14½ft) deep and is a remnant of the Ice Age, dammed by a glacial moraine. It is gradually silting up, so do the walk while it's still here. This is a very pretty, reedy tarn, surrounded by conifers and overlooked by Tarn Crags on the far side. You will join a forest track and will see a sign immediately in front of you. Go right (the 'White route') and after 100m (110yd) or so the conifers will give way to a short section of birch trees. Harrop Tarn is fairly small and after another 100m (110yd) you will have passed the head of it.

The track will now take you gently uphill through the forest, accompanied by a gurgling beck on your left. After crossing three small streams, you will come to a path (signed 'Watendlath') which disappears into the trees on your left and would seem to offer all sorts of exciting possibilities. This, however, is for real mountain men (and women), so anyone else should keep following the track to a T-junction. Turn right, alongside another small beck which comes crashing down a small outcrop of rock on your left. Surrounded by larch, this is very pretty in autumn.

After another 100m (110yd) or so, you will come to another junction and a superb view over the trees to the summit of Helvellyn. A logging track swings right. If no stalkers are about, it is worth a swift diversion to the top of Swithin Crag – the rocky knoll in front of you, just above the curve of the logging track. From the crag you will have a terrific panorama of Thirlmere valley, with Combe Gill and Nethermost Pike directly in front of you.

Continue along the main track, past a track joining from the left, and you will then begin the slow descent. You will lose sight of Helvellyn as the trees close in around you and the hillside drops away steeply on the right. The track drops to a gate. Note the extension bolted on to the top of the gate to keep in the deer. Once through, you will have another good view of Helvellyn and Thirlmere. Cragsteads Gill crashes down the rocks on your left, passing under the track.

The official white route swings right here, going down a narrow path along the edge of the forestry plantation. This makes a steep descent to the road and a walk back to Dobgill car park. Ignore it, and continue down the track across open fell, enjoying the views. The track zigzags down to another gate and you will then be back in the forest again. Eventually you will arrive down at the road. Go left along it for 125m (135yd) or so and you will come to a cutting, where the road has been blasted through an outcrop of rock. There are three gates on the right-hand side of the road. You will be going through the first (signed 'Dobgill'), but go first to the far side of the outcrop and through the gate, which will lead you to the top of the rock and the view. This is Hause Point, and until the

early 1980s it was one of the few access points to Thirlmere – all 20m (22yd) of it. Things have certainly improved since then.

Go through the gate (signed 'Dobgill') and enjoy the lovely wooded shore walk. After 1km (⅔ mile) of blissful, easy walking, you will pass a rocky promontory. I defy any reader to resist the temptation to go to the end of this and look at the view. Shortly after this, the path begins to wind inland, skirting the end of Dob Gill as it joins Thirlmere. Walk up the marshy field to a kissing gate and you will rejoin the road opposite Dobgill car park. If you have parked here, you are at your walk's end. If your car is at Steel End, turn left along the road and retrace the outward route to the start of the walk.

VISITOR ATTRACTIONS

The nearest visitor attractions are in Grasmere (see Walk 20: Rydal Water & Grasmere) and Keswick (see Walk 10: River Greta).

Combe Gill and Nethermost Pike seen from a point between Steel End and Dob Gill

20 RYDAL WATER & GRASMERE

PARKING AND START/FINISH
The walk starts from the National Park Authority car park at Pelter Bridge, just off the A591, south of Rydal Hall (GR 365060). Space is limited

DISTANCE
7km (4½ miles)

TERRAIN
Easy walking, some of it uphill to begin with and then a gentle stroll back

Rydal Water and Grasmere are the classic English lakes. This walk begins with a climb to Loughrigg Terrace for a wonderful view of Grasmere, before dropping to the lakeshore and coming back along the River Rothay and the shores of Rydal Water. The route out takes the very best advantage of the views and you are accompanied by water all the way back.

URNING left out of the car park, the lane heads away from the bridge past Cote How Guest House, a pair of Lakeland stone cottages and a short terrace. The tarmac ends at a wooden farm gate. Go through the gap alongside and continue along the rough track to another gate. As you go through the gate, the bridleway will be signed right, along the shore, but your route continues straight on, along the upper path. Pause at the wooden bench and take in the view of Rydal Water, with its two small islands. This is a pretty little lake, despite the proximity of the A591 along its eastern shore. Once known as Rothaymere (after the river which flows through), it is less than 1.2km (¾ mile) long by 0.4km (¼ mile) wide and only around 16 metres (52ft) deep. It is very popular for swimming and, being comparatively shallow, doesn't take too long to warm up in summer.

The track will lead you past the lake and alongside a stone wall, losing the view behind the trees. Follow the fence line and you will cross a small beck and climb to the first of Rydal caves. These are actually old slate quarries. You can just about scramble into the first one, but it is wet and dark so there is not a great deal to see. Getting down from the cave will seem a lot more difficult than the 2m (6½ft) climb up.

Continue along the path and climb up the side of a slate tip to a small plateau and the second of the caves. This is much bigger – in fact, whole choirs from Charlotte Mason College have been known to sing Christmas carols in here! Recently, however, the roof has been subject to rock fall and at the time of writing the cave entrance is fenced off. Do not enter. The route continues past the cave and up a slight rise to a good viewpoint, taking in Rydal

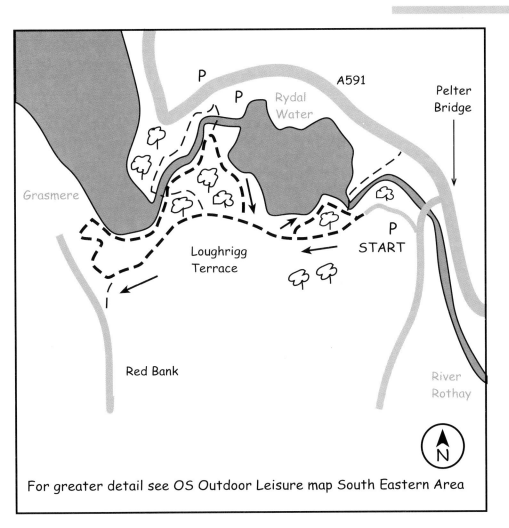

P

P

Rydal
Water

A591

Pelter
Bridge

Grasmere

Loughrigg
Terrace

P
START

Red Bank

River
Rothay

N

For greater detail see OS Outdoor Leisure map South Eastern Area

Water on your right and looking across the lake to Nab Scar and, below it, Nab Cottage.

🔎 *In an area seething with Wordsworth associations, it should come as no surprise to discover that Nab Cottage also has literary connections. Built as a farmhouse in 1702, it was once the home of Thomas De Quincey, famous for his book* Confessions of an English Opium Eater. *He first came to Grasmere in 1807, specifically to visit his great hero, Wordsworth. He stayed with the family at Dove Cottage for several months, and when they moved out to Allan Bank, Thomas took over the tenancy. While living at Dove Cottage, he courted Margaret Simpson, whose father owned Nab Farm (as it was then called). Wordsworth thought De Quincey should not marry such a 'low-born' woman and wrote complaining letters to De Quincey's mother. It didn't work: Thomas married Margaret in 1817. In 1829 he*

A superb view of Rydal Water from Loughrigg Terrace, below Ewe Crag

bought the farm from her father and moved in. He kept on Dove Cottage for another 10 years to store his vast library of books. Nab Cottage is now a guest house.

I have to admit to a great liking for De Quincey, and when work-ing at Dove Cottage as a guide I used to vary the routine with occasional De Quincey tours. His Recollections of the Lake Poets *brings the Wordsworths' Grasmere years vividly to life and should be required reading before visiting Dove Cottage.*

Leaving this vantage point, head along the path, winding around the side of Loughrigg (ignore the path beaten through the brack-en on the right). The path goes to the left of a small conifer plan-tation and then forks. Go left again, on the narrower path, climbing steeply on to Loughrigg Terrace. This is a superb viewpoint, which just gets better and better. Turn left, and as you walk along the terrace you will see Grasmere coming into view, above it the dis-tinctive cone of Helm Crag and, to the right, Dunmail Raise – the U-shaped saddle between Helm Crag and Fairfield.

🔊 *There are several variations on the origin of the name Grasmere. The popular one is that it is Old English for 'the lake with the grassy shore'. More likely, it derives from the Viking settlers, who kept pigs in the surrounding woods and would have known it as Grismere, 'griss' being Scandinavian for 'pig'.*

Pig Lake is very pretty, surrounded by high fells and with an island almost exactly in the centre. On a still autumn morning, the setting is perfect. The lake and island are owned by the National Trust and the island's stone barn used to be used for sheltering sheep (which were brought across in flat-bottomed boats). The lake is 1.6km (1 mile) long by 0.8km (½ mile) wide and around 22m (72ft) deep.

Dunmail Raise is named after the last King of Cumberland, supposedly buried here after his defeat by the Saxon King Edmund, in 945 AD. In fact, he is rumoured to have died on a pilgrimage to Rome nearly 30 years later. The Raise marks the boundary between the old counties of Cumberland and Westmorland.

You will pass a number of wooden seats along the terrace. At the fourth, pause for a rest and enjoy the view. Just visible over Dunmail is the summit of Blencathra. Follow the view around to the left and the dull yellow building below Helm Crag is Allan Bank, one of Wordsworth's three Grasmere homes.

🕭 *Allan Bank is highly visible from most of the surrounding fells. It was this fact that led Wordsworth to call it as 'a temple of abomination' when it was built in 1805 by a Liverpool merchant named Crump. Three years later, when the Wordsworths had outgrown the accommodation at Dove Cottage, Allan Bank proved the only house in Grasmere large enough to take them all. Wordsworth lived there for nearly three years, but the chimneys smoked and the rooms were cold, so as soon as the rectory became available the family moved out. The house is now owned by the National Trust and rented privately.*

Looking down from Loughrigg Terrace over Banerigg Woods and Grasmere

The path now drops down to cross a small beck and will then bring you to a pair of gates. Go through the kissing gate and turn immediately right through another kissing gate (signed 'Grasmere'). This takes you into Deerbolts Wood, once part of High Close estate (High Close House is now a youth hostel). The path slopes gently downhill, taking you through a delightful mixed woodland full of traditional English trees such as beech, sycamore and larch. After a few minutes' steady descent, you will arrive at the National Trust warden's cottage. Turn sharp right (signed 'Lake, White Moss & Rydal') and follow the path down through the woods to Grasmere shore.

As you approach the stone wall at the boundary of the woods, you will see two gates. Go through the left-hand one on to the shore and enjoy a paddle along the shingle beach. There is a lovely view of the valley, and the grassy bank is an ideal picnic spot. Follow the shore along to the wooden footbridge, just past the weir. Do not cross the bridge, but continue on the path alongside the clear river, heading downstream towards another wood. Keep an eye out for kingfishers along here.

After four or five minutes you will go through a kissing gate and into another wood. Pass through another kissing gate and climb the path above the river. The rush of water is very encouraging and drowns out most of the surrounding sound, apart from the occasional fighter plane. Keep to the riverbank and the path will bring you to another footbridge. There are two reasons why you might want to cross here: the public toilets, and the ice-cream van which invariably stands in White Moss car park, on the far side of the A591 road.

If neither of these strike you as particularly compelling, turn right here and follow the path away from the bridge. (As a third alternative, you could continue straight on at the bridge and follow the path along a wetland conservation area walkway. If so, keep dogs on leads, particularly in spring when you might disturb nesting waterfowl.) The path heads uphill (signed 'Loughrigg Terrace' and brings you to yet another kissing gate in a stone wall. Go through it, turn left and keep to the stone wall. The path will eventually bring you back to Rydal Water, dropping down to the lake shore and a very pleasant stroll along the water's edge.

Finally you will run out of beach and come to yet another kissing gate in a stone wall. Go through it and follow the path through Rydal Woods. You will leave the woods via a nice old iron kissing gate and find yourself in a field at the foot of Rydal Water. Follow the clear path across the field and alongside the Rothay again (the river effectively links Grasmere and Rydal to Windermere). After a couple of minutes you will approach a footbridge, which leads up to the road. Do not cross the bridge, but turn right and follow the less distinct path up the field to another kissing gate. Once through, you will be in the woods again. Continue uphill, up 12 steps and through a final gate, to emerge on the tarmac lane from Pelter Bridge. Then turn right and retrace your steps to the start of the walk.

VISITOR ATTRACTIONS

Dove Cottage
Town End, Grasmere
Tel: 015394 35544
William Wordsworth's most famous home, where he lived while at the height of his powers as a poet. Almost all the furniture belonged to Wordsworth, and the house and garden have been restored to how they were in Wordsworth's day. There are guided tours of the house and an excellent museum. There is a restaurant on site.

Rydal Mount
Rydal, Nr Ambleside
Tel: 015394 33002
Wordsworth's final home; he died here in 1850. There are very attractive grounds and a view which has hardly changed since the poet lived here.

21 ELTERWATER

PARKING AND START/FINISH
The walk starts from the National Trust car park in Elterwater village centre. Get there early as it fills very quickly, largely due to the immense popularity of the nearby Britannia Inn

DISTANCE
8.25km (5 miles)

TERRAIN
Easy walking, some across fields which will probably be muddy in winter. Very little climbing and a number of shortcut points

Elterwater is an old Norse name meaning 'the lake of the swans'. It is not as dramatic as some of the major lakes, but can be the focus of several superb low-level walks. This is a walk across gentle countryside which includes two small waterfalls: Colwith Force and Skelwith Force.

FROM the car park, head out to the road and turn left over the road bridge. Follow the road, taking the opportunity to enjoy the views across the fields to the lake. This is a relatively quiet stretch of country lane but there are a number of blind corners, so take care. You'll be on the road for about 1km (⅔ mile).

Beyond the youth hostel (originally a seventeenth-century farmhouse) and Elterwater Country House Hotel (the latter now owned by the Langdale timeshare complex) there is a long, uninhabited stretch before passing the entrance to a house on your left. About 50m (54yd) beyond that, you will see a sign on your right for Fletcher's Wood, a National Trust-owned woodland. Climb over the stile and a path will lead you through the trees past oak, birch and the occasional larch.

The path leads to another stile. Cross over and continue up a field – keeping the stone wall to your right – to a vehicle track.

The upper falls at Colwith Force, sheltered by trees in a rocky ravine

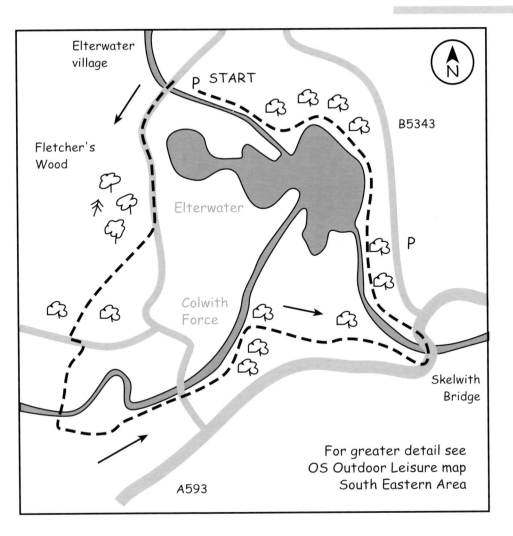

Turn right along it. Go through the first white farm gate, just past
a barn, and continue along the track until a white house comes
into sight on your right. Look out for a stile and footpath sign in
the stone wall on your left. Cross the stile into a field, and follow
the wall on your right. This little diversion takes you around the
house and grounds. Keep to the field boundary and you will be on
the correct route. At the corner of the field, cross the stone wall
via the next stile and then bear slightly to the right, through a gap
in another stone wall.

The route goes left here, but before you head downhill go
across to the farm gate in the wall in front of you for an excellent
view of Wetherlam. Then head down the field. The path is indistinct, so keep to the wall on your right and you will come to a
wooden farm gate in the corner of the field. The way this gate is

hinged into the wall is pretty interesting, using the stone wall as part of the hinge.

Go through the gate and turn right: then, as soon as you have crossed the beck, bear left and follow the beck downhill for 20m (22yd) or so. The path then bears away from the beck, heading across the field towards a neat black-and-white farmhouse. The path forks left just before the farm, taking you to a stile in the wire fence. Once over, you will be on a gravelled drive next to Irving Howe farm. Go left down the drive to the road. Turn right along the road and you will be heading into Little Langdale. There is a wonderful view of Wetherlam across the fields to your left. The road along here is very narrow so watch out for cars, especially in summer – visitors seem to find the stone walls strangely intimidating and tend to drive in the middle of the road. (Watch out also for the sign on the gate of Green Bank Cottage: 'Never mind the dog, beware the owner'.

You will now walk past a terrace of houses and, just after Lang Parrock, should look out for a narrow kissing gate on the left, just by the parking space for Greenbank terrace. The gate has a sign which reads 'Please keep in single file, growing crop, herb-rich meadow'. Before you go through, bear in mind that if any members of the party feel tired and thirsty, the Three Shires Inn is just a few hundred metres further along the road.

Go through the gate and head straight across the field to the far corner (the footpath is very clear). Cross the narrow wooden footbridge over Greenburn Beck and bear right, then follow the path towards the white farmhouse at the top of the field. The path runs between a wire fence and a stone wall, past the front of Stang End farm and out on to a tarmac lane. Turn left and you will immediately come to a sign and a fork in the road. Go left, signed 'Colwith' and 'Skelwith'. This is an extremely narrow lane, so if a car approaches be prepared to leap nimbly into the adjoining field. As you stroll along, enjoy the views to the left across a field to the Three Shires Inn; it's too late to go back to it now.

Within minutes, you should arrive at High Park farm. There is a public footpath through the farmyard to a wooden gate, which takes you into a field. The path goes straight across to the kissing gate in the wall ahead. Once beyond the wall you should turn left and follow the path to another gate, which takes you into the woods. The path forks immediately. Go left – signed 'Colwith Force (permissive path)' – down through the trees, towards the sound of rushing water.

Eventually you will come to a wide river which winds through the wood. The path follows the river downstream and after a few minutes will bring you to a superb view of Colwith Force, a 21m (68ft) cascade sheltered by trees in a rocky ravine. Continue going downstream, following the clearly defined path through the trees. Eventually you will come to a road. Colwith Bridge, on your left, stands on the old county boundary between Lancashire and Westmorland. However, you should go right, along the road for 100m (110yd) or so.

Just past a lay-by and bridge, you will see a stile in the stone wall on your left, signed 'Skelwith bridge'. Go through and follow the path across the field to the woods to rejoin the river. Just inside the wood, cross the stile and climb steeply up the bank. Carry on up to a wire fence and then follow the path left along it to a stile. This takes you into a field and gives you a view of Loughrigg. Walk across the field and through a metal kissing gate beside Low Park house. Cross straight over the drive, climb a narrow stile and walk down a path between two walls. This will take you to another stile, and then across another field to yet another stile.

You will now come to Park Farm. Look for the yellow marker arrow on the side of one of the stone barns – the route goes between the buildings and down a vehicle track. Walk past the static caravans and through the gate and keep to the vehicle track, passing a small wood on your right. At the end of the track, on the far side of the field, you will come to Park House and the centre of some controversy. At the time of writing, although the right of way goes through the grounds of Park House, there is a permissive path which diverts you around the garden. Be kind and follow the permissive path: the owners of Park House have enough people going through their garden without adding to their number. The track then takes you past a house called Tiplog and through a gateway. About 20m (22yd) beyond the gate, watch out for a marker post on your left and take the path left, across an open field.

Another kissing gate will take you into Bridge Howe Coppice and towards a wooden bungalow. Fork right, around the bungalow to a wooden kissing gate. This will take you through and on to the tarmac road. Turn left and follow the road around the corner and over the bridge. Just past here is the entrance to Kirkstone Slate Gallery and car park.

Kirkstone Slate Gallery has a superb café and shop, and the slate works behind fashions the local green-blue slate. This is exported around the world, and in the gallery you can buy anything in slate from an ashtray to a fireplace.

The route goes through the gallery car park (signed 'Public footpath to Elterwater'). Where the tarmac drive forks by Riverside Cottage, go right, through the slate works and into the trees beside the River Brathay. You have now left all roads behind so dogs can safely be unleashed. The path leads upstream, past the small but vigorous waterfall. For a good look at this, cross over the two iron footbridges built on the rocks in the middle of the river. At only 6m (19ft) high, this isn't the most impressive waterfall in the Lake District, although it does lay claim to having the highest volume of falling water, which is due to the large catchment area of the surrounding fells.

The path will bring you to a kissing gate and into another field. Walk straight across, heading to the left of the clump of trees ahead of you. This is a pleasant wide expanse after all the woods and narrow lanes. As you follow the broad river, the view of the Langdale Pikes will open up in front of you. Beyond the trees, go through a farm gate and keep following the river. As you approach the next gate and the wood, you will reach the foot of Elterwater and a classic view across the water to the mountains. Elterwater is

the smallest of the 16 lakes, being less than 1km (⅔ mile) long and only 15m (48ft) at its deepest point.

Walk into the woods and follow the footpath around the edge of the lake. This is a lovely wood in spring, when it is a mass of bluebells. The path winds around to the left, following a wire fence as you lose sight of the lake and crossing a wooden footbridge. You will now be beside the river once more and there is a very easy, level path which will take you straight back to the car park at Elterwater village.

VISITOR ATTRACTIONS

For attractions in Ambleside, see Walk 20: Rydal Water & Grasmere or Walk 3: Stockghyll Force.

Swans on Elterwater, with the snow-capped Langdale Pike beyond

22 ULLSWATER

PARKING AND START/FINISH
The walk starts from the Ullswater steamers car park at Glenridding (south side of the village on the A592 – GR 390169)

DISTANCE
10.5km (6½ miles)

TERRAIN
Level walking for most of the way, with some short uphill sections

Ullswater is arguably the most attractive of the 16 lakes. The second longest, it lies in the heart of dramatic scenery and does not suffer the noise and visitor pressure which plague Windermere. The south-eastern shore has no roads, no traffic and very little habitation. You are in wild and lovely countryside with the prospect of a steamer trip back to the car.

Although this route is commonly walked in reverse, I am a firm believer in dispensing with the slog along the road as quickly as possible. However, this does mean that you should give yourself plenty of time to complete the walk – and don't aim for last steamer of the day. If you miss it, you will have a long walk back.

ONCE you have armed yourself with a timetable from the steamer ticket office, head back across the car park and go through the farm gate by the road entrance. This leads into a field for a nice stroll along the lakeshore. It will bring you out at the A592 next to a convenient snack bar. Before crossing, if you look left along the road you can see St Patrick's Well in the stone wall.

Patterdale – St Patrick's Valley – is named after the sixth-century saint who brought Christianity to the area. St Patrick's church (see below) is a Victorian building.

Cross the road to a set of steps directly opposite (signed 'Permissive path to Patterdale') and follow the path left, parallel to the road. This avoids a few hundred metres of pavement. You will come back to the road at the entrance to Patterdale Hall estate. Cross over again and there is another short section of off-road footpath before you will be forced to walk along the pavement, heading in the direction of Patterdale village.

After 350m (380yd), you will pass St Patrick's church and the rectory and come to a turning on your left, beside a stone-built hall (look for the Club Alpine Swiss sign, dating from 1863). Turn left down the lane, signed 'To Howtown & Boredale'. The track leads you across the fields to Side Farm which, if you are already flagging, sells ice creams. Walk into the farmyard and at the top, by the shop, turn left, signed 'Howtown & Sandwick'. Go through the farm gate and follow the track.

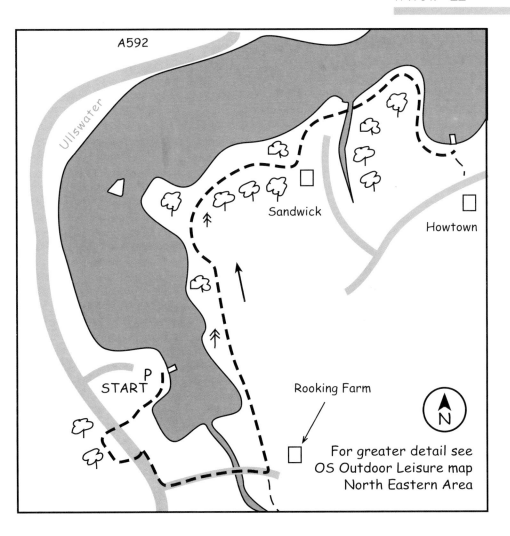

There is a good view left of Glenridding and Helvellyn, although photographers may grumble about the ugly iron farm shed in the middle distance. From this point you can see Dollywagon Pike, High Crag and the western tip of St Sunday Crag. You are now on a very easy track, the fellside rising up on your right and an increasingly good view of Ullswater on your left. You will occasionally see red squirrels in the trees along here and you might encounter groups of pony trekkers from Side Farm.

When you have been walking for about 50 minutes, the wall will start to drop away to your left and you will climb a short rise. Suddenly, you will have the most magnificent view of the lake, with Norfolk Island in the centre, green rolling fells on the far side, a mighty Scots pine on your left ... this is an ideal spot for an enjoyable picnic.

🐾 *Ullswater is named after another of the ubiquitous Norse settlers, in this case L'Ulph, the first Lord of Ullswater. The lake is one of four in the Lake District designated a public highway – the others are Derwent Water, Coniston Water and Windermere. Speed restrictions imposed by the National Park Authority in 1983 keep the lake clear of power boats and water skiers. The lake is 12km (7½ miles) long by 1.2km (¾ mile) wide, and is 62.4m (203ft) at its deepest point.*

The track narrows to a path here and this is a lovely part of the walk. The view of the lake is a constant companion. On the far shore you may be able to spot a square grey tower rising above the trees. This is Lyulph's Tower, in Gowbarrow Park, just east of Aira Force. Its name is another reference to the first Lord of Ullswater,

A view from below Place Fell across to Glenridding and the steamer pier

although in this case the connection is rather more distant: the tower was built as a hunting lodge in the nineteenth century by the Duke of Norfolk.

The path runs about 20m (65ft) above the lake and unfortunately there is no clear route down to the lake itself through the bracken. Occupy yourself instead with spotting the different tree species (which include beech, sycamore, willow, rowan and juniper) until you get to Silver Point. This is a distinct promontory, and if you divert to the tip you will have an excellent view north and south, along Ullswater.

The path along here undulates, with a steep uphill pull now and again. For the most part, you will probably feel completely

isolated. The fellside rises above you on the left, from time to time covered in mixed woodland. Depending on the time of day you set off, you should be well into the walk before you begin encountering fellow walkers who are doing the route from the Howtown direction. If you were doing the same, you could now be stuck behind them all – a particular problem as everyone piles off the steamer at Howtown and queues to go through the kissing gate at the start of the walk.

You will eventually drop down through the woods to approach a drystone wall and Scalehow Beck. The path curves around the corner of the field boundary and you will drop down to cross the beck via a wooden footbridge. The route continues on the other side, but it is worth diverting upstream to find Scalehow Force, an attractive waterfall hidden in the trees.

From the footbridge, continue along the main path. You will now have fields and the stone wall between the path and the lake, although there are still good views down to it. Keep to the wall and the path will bring you down to the tiny hamlet of Sandwick. When you reach the tarmac road, turn left past Bushey Cottage and Beckside Farm, and follow the lane through the wooden farm gate and over the wooden vehicle bridge. The lane becomes a track which will lead you through the field to another farm gate. Your route goes right here (signed 'Public footpath') off the track and along the drystone wall, past a ruined building. According to a local farmer I met, this pile of stones was once a ferryman's cottage. It seemed the farmer didn't value it too highly as a site of great historical interest: he was busy recycling the stones for the upkeep of his walls.

The path will take you through another gate and across an open field, with a lovely view ahead of the tree-lined lake shore. Once through two more gates, the path rejoins the lakeshore. Keep to the wall and another gate will lead you into Hallinhag Wood, a delightful mixed woodland which runs right down to the shore-line. The wood lies on the flanks of Hallin Fell, and as you round the hillside and leave the wood behind, you will be able to see the northern end of Ullswater. The distinctive cone at Pooley Bridge is Dunmallard Hill, the site of a Iron Age hill fort and Pooley Bridge's first settlement.

The path now begins to drop you gently towards the shore and you will overlook Howtown Wyke ('wyke' is the local name for bay). Keep your eyes open for the steamers coming into the pier; from the south, they pass right below your viewpoint. A bench seat is thoughtfully provided.

♪ *The Ullswater Navigation and Transit Company began running boats on Ullswater in 1855. The present two craft are over 100 years old:* Lady of the Lake *was launched in 1877 and* Raven *in 1889. They*

were originally steam driven but were converted to diesel in the 1930s. The journey from Howtown to Glenridding takes about 35 minutes, and if it's blowing a gale, each launch has a welcoming bar below deck.

A yacht sailing on Ullswater off Skelly Neb, near Howtown

Setting off again, you will pass the edge of a field boundary and the garden to Waternook House and drop down to a kissing gate. Walk down the steps, and a made path will then bring you back along the lakeshore. Follow the shore around to the small wood, and at the footbridge go left to the pier. Alternatively, if you keep going straight you will come to the road. Turn right, and five minutes' walking will bring you to the Howtown Hotel, which does teas and has a public bar for walkers at the rear of the hotel. Don't get too settled, though – keep an eye on the steamer timetable!

VISITOR ATTRACTIONS

Dalemain, Penrith
Tel: 017684 86450
A large, Georgian-fronted house with interesting architecture and family history. There are also fascinating gardens and a superb tea shop in the baronial hall.

Ullswater Navigation and Transit Company
Glenridding Pier,
Glenridding, Ullswater
Tel: 017684 82229
Cruises from Glenridding, Howtown and Pooley Bridge.

23 CRUMMOCK WATER & MOSEDALE BECK

PARKING AND START/FINISH
The walk starts from Lanthwaite Wood National Trust pay-and-display car park (GR 149215), 1.5km (1 mile) east of Loweswater village

DISTANCE
10.5km (6½ miles)

TERRAIN
Level walking along the shore of Crummock Water, with a long, slow climb to Scale Force and the back of Mellbreak, and a gentle descent. The going is good under-foot but may be wet, especially around the pumping station

This is a terrific walk which takes in a variety of spectacular views, including Criffel and the Solway Firth. Crummock Water is long and peaceful and has a distinct atmosphere all of its own. You can make a complete circuit of the lake, but the eastern shore is rather spoilt for walkers by the presence of the B5289. The western shore is wilder and more isolated, and this route gives you the opportunity to visit Scale Force, the Lake District's longest waterfall.

THE start of this walk is ideal: you spurn the road and head off immediately into Lanthwaite Wood. Leave the car park via the wooden gate (at the opposite end to the entrance) and follow the forestry track through the trees. You will be accompanied on your right by the sound of water from Cocker Beck, which flows from Crummock Water across Lorton Vale to Cockermouth, where it joins the River Derwent and flows out to sea at Workington, on the west coast.

Ignore the waymarked path which goes off to the left (a rather energetic route up Whiteside) and continue straight along the track, passing two more forks left (one of which has a barrier across it). This will bring you to the shingle beach at the foot of Crummock Water and an excellent view of Mellbreak. This is an atmospheric spot, dominated by a tall Scots pine, with a tremendous sweeping view of the lake and surrounding fells.

Crummock Water is a Celtic name, appropriate for a lake which is so strongly reminiscent of a Scottish loch. The name means 'the bent or curved lake'. Crummock Water is 4km (2½ miles) long by less than 1km (⅔ mile) wide. At the deepest point it is 44m (144ft). The lake is owned by the National Trust.

The path forks here. Go right and you will immediately encounter the concrete dam wall and the weir. Cross over the two foot-bridges which span the weir. The second bridge feels very precari-ous, a sensation heightened by the tremendous rush of water pass-ing underneath. Once on the other side of the river, you will be embarking on a lovely walk along the edge of the lake and through a small wood, with terrific views of Mellbreak, Whiteside and the

P START

For greater detail see
OS Outdoor Leisure map
North Western Area

Park Beck

River Cocker

N

Mellbreak

Low Ling Crag

Crummock
Water

Scale Force

Mosedale Beck

lower flanks of Grasmoor. The path runs alongside the concrete
dam wall, crosses Park Beck and then arrives at the pumping station, built by Workington Corporation in 1903. Continue along the
edge of the dam; depending on recent weather, you may have to
walk along the top of the dam to avoid the waterlogged marsh on
your right. Fortunately, the lake is less than a metre deep at this
point, so it is not too intimidating. The wall ends at a wooden
fence. Cross the stile and continue through the field, keeping to
the shore.

The path now climbs above the level of the lake past hawthorn,
birch and rowan. The conical fell you can see on the far shore
is Rannerdale Knotts, and just beyond it is the wonderfully
named High Snockrigg. The sharp, triangular peak to the left of
Rannerdale is Whiteless Pike.

The views get better and better. The path will lead you across a shingle shore, through a kissing gate and out of the field via a stile (note the dog hole alongside). You now have a lovely bracken-covered field on your right, which sweeps up the lower flanks of Mellbreak. There are a number of fast-flowing becks coming down Mellbreak, but the extraordinary thing is how few of them you have to cross: most of them just soak into the ground. This makes the going very marshy in winter, so you may feel like climbing higher or sticking closer to the shore.

After 1.5km (1 mile) of steady walking along the shoreline you will approach the very impressive odd-shaped peninsula of Low Ling Crag on your right. This is a real post-Ice Age oddity – a *roches moutonnées*, to give the proper term. Divert down to stand at the end and take in the tremendous all-round views.

Mature trees in Lanthwaite Wood at the start of the walk

The spectacular Scale Force plummets through a narrow cleft in the rock face

From the crag, continue along the shore for another 200m (220yd) or so and the path will then begin to head inland. You will cross a couple of smaller becks and then arrive at Scale Beck. Head right and follow the beck upstream, without crossing the wooden footbridge. Climb to a wire fence and walk between the fence and the river, as far as a wooden footbridge. In theory, you should cross the stile here and head up the fell, along the old bridleway to Ennerdale. But this would involve missing Scale Force, so at the expense of a little tricky navigation later on, continue uphill, beside the river. In fact, at this point you will be walking between two rivers, formed by a rocky moraine.

133

After about 100m (110yd) you will be able to see the waterfall, just visible in the patch of trees ahead and to your left. As you join the fence line again, go left across the wooden footbridge and walk the few metres upstream to Scale Force. This is a very picturesque spot. The 52m (170ft) waterfall plummets through a narrow cleft in the rock face, surrounded by a copse of trees. It is a double cascade and with care you can walk into the cleft, right up to the lower cascade. (In fact, if conditions are right, you can climb to the foot of the upper cascade, but I am not going to recommend it.) Emerging from the cleft, you will be faced with an expansive view across Crummock Water to Whiteless, Grasmoor and Whiteside. Walk back to the footbridge. The route you want to follow goes up along the fence line, to climb the back of Mellbreak. There isn't a distinct footpath, although there is a stile halfway along the fence. If conditions are right, go to the corner of the fence, cross the beck and climb alongside the fence. Alternatively, if it is very boggy, bear left and curve around as soon as you can to rejoin the fence higher up. There are several paths, which makes things a little confusing. Stay in sight of the fence and you will be going in the right general direction.

The 155m (505ft) summit of Mellbreak is fenced because the fell is in private ownership. Many regard fencing-in a Lakeland peak as highly controversial, although a few stiles are provided to cross it. As you climb you will be able to look back to Crummock Water and, beyond, to the road from Newlands Valley as it drops down to Buttermere.

At the top of the fenced boundary, another fence comes in from the left. Go through the gate and walk straight ahead, over a boggy section at the back of Mellbreak. You will now lose the views to Crummock and this wide, open moorland is very windswept and isolated. The path leads straight across the marsh to a mystery metal gate. The fence here has long since gone, so actually going through the gate would be obsessive. Instead, pause and look north east to see Criffel and the Solway Firth. It is also worth keeping your eyes open for kestrels along this section of the walk.

From the mystery gate, the path gently descends a pleasant green fellside, heading towards the distant river. Crossing a couple of smaller becks, you will eventually arrive at another fence line, between you and Mosedale Beck. Follow the track downhill and see how much you can remember from school geography lessons about oxbow bends: Mosedale Beck has some good examples. This valley was once mined for lead – there is an old mine shaft on the far side of the valley. The last mine closed in the 1890s.

Passing a small cairn and an old stone wall, you will come to what appears to be a brick water tank. Just above this on the fellside is a deep hole, which I like to think is probably a boggart den.

🐾 *The boggart is a very rare Lakeland beast, comprising half fox and half badger. There are two varieties; one has the front half of a fox and the back half of a badger, the other the reverse. Sightings are very rare and you usually only see the back half as the animal disappears over a wall. If you don't believe me, a fine example is exhibited in a glass case in the Twa Dogs Inn, Keswick.*

This is a nice, easy descent which will give you plenty of opportunity to take in the views. The route eventually forks at the apex of a triangular plantation of fir trees. To the left is the main track, which would bring you down at Loweswater village. However, you still have interesting things to explore, so take the path to the right of the plantation, keeping to the fence line. This way you will get a good view of the end of Mellbreak, a towering crag which looms on your right. You may also catch a glimpse of Loweswater and the village through the trees on your left, and a view of Whiteless ahead of you. When you pass through the stone wall, there will be a better view of Loweswater. Don't leave it too long after the publication date of this book before doing this walk, however, as the view is due to be interrupted by the spruce plantation on the other side of the wall. For the time being the trees are young enough not to get in the way.

This is a very pretty, sheltered section of the walk. The path drops down to Green Wood, an ancient sessile oak woodland. At the corner of the stone wall, the path then does loop which will bring you left, back to the bottom of the wall and a wooden farm gate. As you make the loop, you will get a glimpse of Whiteless and Crummock Water. Walk through the gate and along the narrow track between the walls. This will all feel very unexplored along here. Keep to the track and it will take you between a group of houses to a T-junction with a tarmac lane.

According to the wonderfully optimistic Ordnance Survey, there is a right of way which goes across the fields and back to the lakeshore path from this point. Unless you happen to be wearing waders, however, I do not recommend it. Instead, go left over the road bridge over Park Beck and walk along to the next T-junction. Turn right and walk along the quiet country lane, enjoying yet more views of Whiteless. The lane curves left past Muncaster House to bring you to a crossroads. Turn right, over the bridge, and you will be back at the entrance to Lanthwaite Wood car park.

VISITOR ATTRACTIONS

For the nearest attractions, see Walk 18: Loweswater.

24 DERWENT WATER

PARKING AND START/FINISH
The walk starts from the pay-and-display car park at Keswick boat landings

Known to many as the Queen of the Lakes, Derwent Water offers magnificent opportunities for waterside walking. There is a route which completely circles the lake and is for the most part right on the lakeshore. Add superb mountain scenery, delightful woodland and the opportunity to catch a lake launch if you get tired, and you have the recipe for a classic walk.

DISTANCE
The complete circuit of the lake is 16km (10 miles). The walk described below omits the final section from Hawes End to Keswick and is 11km (7 miles)

TERRAIN
Level walking throughout

To provide the best views, I have taken a clockwise route around the lake and split the walk into sections, based on the pick-up points for the Derwent Water launches. This means that if you get tired, or simply do not fancy the entire route, you can break the walk with a boat trip.

I have not included the final section of the circuit, from Hawes End back to Keswick: it involves road walking and for the most part is away from the lakeshore. If you insist on completing the circuit, it is not difficult to follow from the map. Otherwise, give it a miss and catch the launch back from Hawes End.

Early morning sun on Cat Bells, seen from Barrow Bay

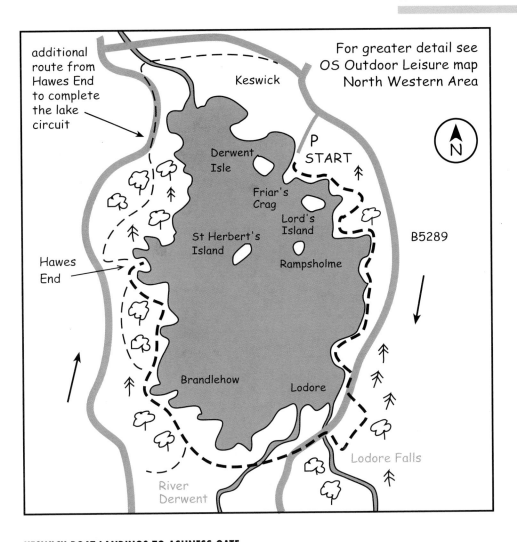

additional route from Hawes End to complete the lake circuit

For greater detail see OS Outdoor Leisure map North Western Area

Keswick

Derwent Isle

P
START

N

Friar's Crag

Lord's Island

St Herbert's Island

Rampsholme

B5289

Hawes End

Brandlehow

Lodore

Lodore Falls

River Derwent

KESWICK BOAT LANDINGS TO ASHNESS GATE

From the car park, you have a choice. If you are feeling anti-social or have dogs (or children) straining to be let off the leash, there is a gate at the far corner of the car park which will take you through the woods to join the walk at Strandshag Bay.

Alternatively, leave the car park and walk along the lane past the boat landings and the National Trust information centre. This is a part of the walk which is popular with Sunday afternoon strollers. As you leave the tarmac and walk through the woods to Friar's Crag, it is not hard to see why it draws so many people. Go past the slate memorial to Ruskin and right to the end of the peninsula for a brilliant view of the lake and the mountains of Borrowdale. You will be able to have a rest on the second best-positioned bench seat in the Lake District.

🔊 *Ruskin is the philosophical father of the National Trust and the slate memorial commemorates his connections with the Lake District. It bears an inscription which reads:*

> *The first thing I remember*
> *as an event in my life was being*
> *taken by my nurse to the brow of*
> *Friar's Crag on Derwentwater*

On the path to Friar's Crag you will pass a memorial to Canon Hardwicke Rawnsley, one of the three founders of the National Trust. The crag was purchased by the Trust in 1922.

Continue around the wooded knoll, go through a gate and follow the path along the shore, through a field. As you approach the wood ahead of you, a path will come in from the left - this is the alternative route from the car park. The path will lead you through a mixed woodland, with glimpses of Castlehead, the wooded hill on your left. There is a rich variety of trees in this boggy wood: look out for Scots pine, oak, yew, beech and alder. It is also a mass of bluebells in spring.

You will eventually emerge from the wood and join a track, which skirts around a field. Turn right and the track will take you past a house (signed 'National Trust Stable Hills Cottage'). Just as a white bungalow comes into sight, there is a path off to the left (signed 'National Trust Footpath'). This follows the lakeshore, with a view of the lake and islands as good as anything seen from Friar's Crag.

🔊 *Derwent Water has four major islands. The nearest to the shore at this point is Lord's Island, once the home of the Earl of Derwent Water (hence the name). The most interesting island - Derwent Isle - lies back towards the boat landings. It was originally called Vicar's Island, but in 1778 was bought by an eccentric individual called Joseph Pocklington. He built a house on the island and then decided to improve the view by constructing a set of follies, including a Druid temple and a stone circle. Guidebook writers of the time referred to it as Pocklington's Island, but were sceptical about the follies; William Gell called them 'an awkward jumble of fantastic gew gaws'.*

The other two islands are Rampsholme and St Herbert's Island. The latter was the hermitage of St Herbert, the close friend and disciple of St Cuthbert. It was a place of pilgrimage in the seventh century, and the embarkation point for monks making the trip to the island was the rocky peninsula south of the boat landings, which is why it is now known as Friar's Crag.

There are also a number of much smaller islands, plus a local oddity known as Floating Island. This is a mass of water plants and vegetation which surfaces in Great Bay, usually around mid-October, buoyed up by marsh gases.

A gate will take you on to another wooded peninsula. The path goes left but a diversion straight on will take you to another seat and view. As you walk back to the path, look on the shore to your right and you will see a large, split boulder. Go and investigate.

🔎 *The inside of this boulder, which is 1m (3ft) in diameter, has been carefully carved and polished. It is an unobtrusive sculpture, which was created and placed here to commemorate the centenary of the National Trust in 1995. It is a beautiful piece of work with strong Celtic resonance, and the effect is of a rock simply sliced open to reveal the sculpture inside. I wonder how many passers-by think that all the rocks around here contain similar weird fossil remains?*

The path now drops down to the pebbled beach and continues along the edge of the lake. This is a terrific part of the route which will take you through an impressive stand of Scots pines. On a good summer day, you can have fun trying to count the tiny figures climbing the ridge of Cat Bells, on the opposite side of the lake. Just before you reach the wooden footbridge, look to the right and you will find a holly which is almost growing out of a Scots pine.

After the footbridge, you will come to a rock outcrop. This will involve a short scramble and I leave you to pick the best route. Once on the top, you will be 6m (20ft) above the lake and walking parallel to the road, which is just the other side of the stone wall. Take care with dogs and children. The path narrows along here and, unless you want to walk along the road, you should follow the path as far as you can and take the first opportunity to drop down to the shore. Continue along the beach to the launch pier at Ashness Gate.

ASHNESS GATE TO LODORE LANDING

Continue past the pier, over a stile and along a pleasant, grassy stretch of shoreline. You will be skirting around Barrow Bay at this point, and as you come to a footbridge, look north for a lovely view towards Skiddaw. As you walk along the far side of the bay, you will be able to see along the shore to the Swiss Lodore Hotel (now called the Stakis Hotel) and, beyond that, to Castle Crag, standing in the Jaws of Borrowdale.

Cross over another stile and walk along a built-up section of path, and you will come to the National Trust Kettlewell car park. If you want to catch the launch at the Lodore landing stage, you simply need to continue along the road for 200m (220yd) or so. Alternatively, cross the road, and go through the gap in the wall, opposite the car park entrance, into Strutta Wood. Follow the path along the fence line to a small gate. Go through and bear right, walking below an ancient scree to another gate. Ignore the path to the left and go through the gate, continuing parallel to the road to

*Reflections in
Great Bay,
Derwent Water*

another path (signed 'Permitted path avoiding road'). This path will take you around a field boundary. Where the path splits, a marker indicates that you should go right. Alternatively, if you go left you will come to Lodore Falls.

🔊 *This is a spectacular 27m (90ft) cataract in a rocky ravine, surrounded by trees and is a real bonus on the walk. It was very popular with the Victorians, who constructed a turnstile to admit visitors. They also kept a small cannon at the hotel and for the equivalent of 20p would fire a blank shot to demonstrate the echo. The waterfall is on land owned by the hotel, hence the honesty box (see page 142).*

Walk back downstream to rejoin the path and cross over a narrow bridge to the back of the Swiss Lodore Hotel. As you reach the

*Manesty Woods,
Derwent Water*

141

drive to the hotel, look out for the honesty box in the back wall of the building. If you have diverted to see the waterfall, put the requested 5p into the box. Then continue to the road and turn left. Note the toilet block on your right – it is the last one you will see until you arrive back at Keswick.

LODORE LANDING TO BRANDLEHOW

About 120m (130yd) along the road you will arrive at a gate and narrow stile, signed 'Public footpath to Manesty'. This next section of the walk is across the flat flood plain at the head of Derwent Water. You will be surrounded by mountains, with a good view along the lake to Skiddaw. Cross the River Derwent via the elegantly arched, 30m (33yd) footbridge and then set off across 300m (330yd) of board walk across the reeds. Note the thoughtfully provided passing places. This board walk is narrow and can be slippery in winter, and as the view is terrific and will probably draw all your attention, it is hard to prevent yourself falling off the boards. Walk past a wooded knoll, through a gate and over more boards to the lakeshore again, to walk around Great Bay.

Just beyond an old stone wall, the path splits. Continue straight on to cross another three sets of board walks, and then the path splits again. Go right and walk around two wooded knolls, right along the lakeshore. Just around the second knoll there is a small, rocky peninsula and what I submit is the best-sited bench in the Lake District. Beat that for a view!

🐾 *Derwent Water is 4.8km (3 miles) long, 1.6km (1 mile) wide and around 22m (72ft) at its deepest point. It is an important area for wildlife conservation with rare fish species, extensive wetlands and important habitats for wildfowl. The lake and River Derwent were given special protected status in spring 1997, when they were designated a Site of Special Scientific Interest. Many experts regard Borrowdale as one of northern Europe's most important examples of a big valley ecosystem.*

Continue along the shore to cross a stile and enter Manesty Woods. The path will lead you through the woods and around Abbot's Bay. Look out for Otter Island – the tiny, wooded island in the centre of the bay.

The path will then bring you to a tarmac track. Go right, past the stone bungalow (signed 'National Trust footpath to Brandlehow') and look out for the slate picnic table in the wood on your right. At the fork in the track, turn left and walk along the rough track to Brandlehow Bay. The path goes right, past Brandlehow House and along the shore. This is a strange section of the shore, with the woods standing on old mine workings. Depending on the recent rainfall, you may be able to keep to the shore all the way around to the landing stage at Brandlehow, in the edge of the woods. If the lake is high, go left at the wire fence and walk uphill to a kissing gate. Then follow the path straight through the woods to the landing stage.

BRANDLEHOW TO HAWES END

There is a choice of route at this point. A higher footpath leads through Brandlehow Park to Hawes End but leaves the lakeshore to do this. (Brandlehow Park was the first property purchased by the National Trust in 1902, just seven years after the Trust was formed. It cost £6500.)

This is a good route, with plenty of features of interest. It makes an excellent walk in its own right, if you catch the launch to Brandlehow. The rickety-looking pier at Brandlehow is an exciting landing point.

However, I recommend keeping to the shoreline wherever possible, so from the landing stage, follow the lower footpath through Brandlehow Woods. The next section of the route is a delightful 1km (⅗ mile) stroll through lovely mixed woodland. After winding around a couple of small bays, you will come to the landing stage at Old Brandlehow. The path forks here. Go left, along the edge of the woods.

The path leads to a fence. Go through the gate and keep right through the field to the Hawes End landing stage. This is a very pretty spot, and an ideal place to rest while you wait for the launch back to Keswick.

VISITOR ATTRACTIONS

Lingholme Gardens
Lingholme, Nr Keswick
Tel: 017687 72003
Magnificent woodlands and a wonderful view of Borrowdale from the north-west corner of Derwent Water.

Derwent Water Launch Company
Lake Side, Keswick
Tel: 017687 72263
The service runs throughout the year, daily except Christmas Day.

For further attractions in Keswick, see Walk 10: River Greta.

Overleaf: *Crossing Morecambe Bay, from Arnside to Grange-over-Sands*

THE COAST

25 MORECAMBE BAY

PARKING AND START/FINISH
This requires meticulous planning and careful co-ordination – or a friend with a second car. Park at Kent's Bank or Grange-over-Sands and take the train to the start of the walk, or park in Arnside and jump on the train at the end

DISTANCE
About 13km (8 miles)

TERRAIN
Completely flat. There is some wading to be undertaken, so shorts and sandals are recommended. Most people do the walk in bare feet. The weather can change quickly out on the Bay, so take warm and windproof layers and a small rucksack to carry your shoes. The walk takes about three hours

This final route is not so much a waterside walk as walking through water – and salt water at that. This is a unique walk, offering a fascinating perspective on the Lakeland fells. It is also unusual in that it should only be done accompanied by the official sands guide, and for this reason I do not offer a route description. *It is extremely dangerous to attempt even part of this walk without the guide.* The bay has numerous quicksands and their positions shift daily.

Shortly before David Ward and I took the guided walk at the end of 1996, the local papers reported a particularly lucky rescue. A man had strolled out on to the sands one evening and nearly drowned, trapped in the quicksand for several hours as the tide rushed in. He was very lucky; by the time the rescue party dug him out, the sea water was lapping at his neck.

If this sounds frightening, good. Go with the guide and you will be perfectly safe.

THIS superb walk is unique, exhilarating and something to tell your friends about when you get home. Guided walks are led across the Morecambe Bay sands by the official guide, Cedric Robinson, and at the time of writing the starting point is outside the Albion Hotel, Arnside.

♠ *The first 'guide to the sands' was appointed in 1326 by the Abbot of Furness, although it is possible that local monks funded an unofficial guide earlier than this. After the dissolution of the monasteries by Henry VIII in 1548, the guide was appointed by the Duchy of Lancaster. It was the guide's duty to pilot coaches across the bay, meeting them at Hest Bank, near Lancaster, and marking out the route with branches of laurel, a practice which continues today. The coming of the Furness railway in 1857 almost put an end to the route, but recreational crossing began to become popular in 1936, after the publication of a series of local newspaper articles. The walks ceased during the World War II, resuming in 1947. Cedric Robinson was appointed as the official guide in the 'Letters Patent under the seals of the Duchy of Lancaster and the County Palatine' in October 1963. He lives at the Guide's Cottage and is a member of HM Coastguard.*

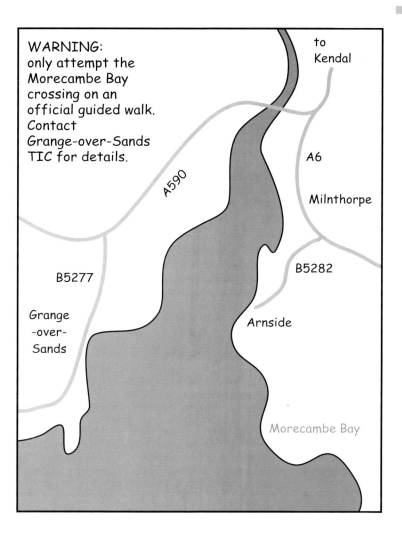

WARNING:
only attempt the
Morecambe Bay
crossing on an
official guided walk.
Contact
Grange-over-Sands
TIC for details.

to
Kendal

A590

A6

Milnthorpe

B5277

B5282

Grange
-over-
Sands

Arnside

Morecambe Bay

You won't be able to miss the start; just look for crowds of people chatting excitedly and wearing odd combinations of fleeces, mountain jackets and sandals. There are often charity groups undertaking the walk, with somebody collecting money before the start. There is also the opportunity to make a donation and buy an official certificate at the end of the walk.

The exact route varies according to the conditions out on the bay. A considerable amount of preparation and experience goes into making sure that the walk is safe and enjoyable on the day. In particular, the channel of the River Kent can alter dramatically and the guide and his assistants mark the route beforehand, planting bushes – known as 'brobs' – to show where it is safe to cross.

Once out on the sands, you will be in a completely different world. Apart from the gaggle of people on the walk, it is isolated and wild. Seagulls wheel overhead and you may spot the occasional fisherman, out on a tractor, preparing nets. The view of the Lakeland fells is particularly striking.

🔾 *In Roman times, Morecambe Bay was a major route into the Lake District. In 1322, Robert the Bruce led his army across the bay and into north Lancashire. As the popularity of the Lakes grew as a tourist destination, coaches began to drive across the bay, many passengers preferring it to the rough, dusty roads – particularly after the introduction of a toll road at Levens Bridge, just south of Kendal. Early coaches were far too heavy and often became bogged down in the sand. The first purpose-built public conveyance was introduced in 1781; this was a 'diligence' or light coach, which could carry three people. The coach company's advertising assured customers that they had 'procured a sober and careful driver who is well acquainted with the sands, and humbly hope that their plan will meet with due encouragement as this is the most cheap, safe and expeditious method of crossing the sands to and from Ulverston.' The coach trip from Lancaster took around two hours and cost five shillings.*

Once you reach the Kent channel, the walk halts. Cedric and his team will check that it is safe to cross and then distribute the group along the channel. The crossing itself can be very exciting, sometimes wading thigh-deep through the strong rush of water, with children racing each other to the other side. Depending on the exact route taken, you may cross the channel several times during the course of the walk.

Across Morecambe Bay, with Arnside in the background

By the time you reach the far side, you will be exhausted but exhilarated. There is usually a scramble for the toilets at Kents Bank, not least to wash the mud off your feet. Don't forget to pick up your signed certificate.

VISITOR ATTRACTIONS
Holker Hall
Cark-in-Cartmel, Grange-over-Sands
Tel: 015395 58328
A superb stately home dating back to the seventeenth century and owned by the Cavendish family. Extensively developed over the past 15 years, there is always a lot going on at Holker. Special events include hot-air ballooning, vintage car rallies (this is also the home of the Lakeland Motor Museum) and birds of prey demonstrations. Pick up a leaflet at Grange tourist information centre, and if you want the place more to yourself, come back and explore the magnificent house and gardens during the week. Very keen to cater for families, the owners have provided a children's playground and a cafeteria on site.

A P P E N D I X 1
MORE WATERSIDE WALKS

Here are 10 suggestions for additional waterside walks, beginning with a round-up of the remaining six lakes.

BASSENTHWAITE LAKE

There are good shorter walks on the eastern shore, particularly around Mirehouse. Park at Dodd Wood car park, walk to the lake shore via St Bega's church and combine the expedition with a visit to Mirehouse (opening times are restricted – contact Keswick tourist information centre for details).

The National Park Authority owns Bassenthwaite Lake and has developed a number of walks along the western and northern shores. Look out for the information boards in the lay-bys.

ENNERDALE WATER

There is a good 11km (7¾ mile) circuit of the lake. Park at Bowness Knott and head off clockwise around the lake. Forest Enterprise have also laid out a Nine Becks walk through the woods. Leaflets are usually available in the car park.

WAST WATER

There is a good circular 12.25km (8½ mile) walk here. Start at the National Trust car park at the head of Wast Water and proceed clockwise around the lake. Don't be put off by the long stretch along the road – it is very quiet and you can amuse yourself spotting the national park logo, formed by the mountains at the head of the lake. The walk along the screes on the eastern shore is particularly exciting and there is an attractive permissive footpath through Low Wood.

ESTHWAITE WATER

Unfortunately, the shoreline is private, with only one short stretch of public access at the northern end of this quiet, pretty lake.

WINDERMERE

This is England's largest lake, but it is curiously frustrating from the point of view of waterside walking. Several shorter walks can be made from various access points – notably at Cockshott Point in Bowness and at Wray Castle on the north-eastern shore. For a longer route, catch a Windermere Lake Steamer from Bowness Bay to Lakeside and walk back along the western shore to Ferry Nab. Catch the car ferry and walk back to Bowness via Cockshott Point.

HAWESWATER

Over the past few years, the National Park Authority has developed an excellent circular walk around the lake. This route is quiet all year round and ideal for hardy, energetic types who want to get right away from it all. The scenery is magnificent. Car parking is rarely a problem, unless the lake level has dropped during a hot summer and the remains of Mardale village have become visible.

The following is a short selection of favourites around tarns, rivers and waterfalls.

ALCOCK TARN, GRASMERE

This is a strenuous but rewarding walk which climbs the side of Rydal Fell to a small, isolated tarn. Continuing the route over Butter Crags and down via Greenhead Gill provides a good tour of Wordsworth country. Walk back via the riverside path through Grasmere village. For a full description, see my *Walker's Companion: Lake District* (Ward Lock, 1994).

WYTHBURN, THIRLMERE

There is a pleasant walk from Steel End farm, Thirlmere, up the eastern bank of the river to the footbridge and then down the western. Good views of Thirlmere open up as you get towards the head of the valley.

LANGSTRATH, BORROWDALE

This is a 9.5km (6 mile) walk in spectacular mountain country, in the heart of Borrowdale. Begin at Stonethwaite, just south of Rosthwaite, and follow the eastern bank of Langstrath Beck past Gallen Force. Cross via the footbridge at the confluence of Langstrath Beck and Stake Beck and return along the lane.

RIVER DUDDON

There are several smaller walks along various parts of the Duddon. They are worth seeking out in order to enjoy the most peaceful of the major Lakeland dales.

BROTHERS WATER

Park at Cow Bridge, Hartsop, just off the A592, then walk anti-clockwise around the tarn. You begin by following Dovedale Beck, an extremely pretty river. The footpath continues over fields to Sykeside Farm, crosses the road and then heads back down to Hartsop via a footpath just off the road. As you approach the tarn again, there is a permitted footpath between it and the road. There are good views on the way back down; however, it's a pity that the road is so close. But for that, the walk would have been one of the main routes in the book.

APPENDIX 2
PUBLIC TRANSPORT

There is no need to feel a second-class citizen in the Lakes just because you do not use a car. Alfred Wainwright researched all his famous guidebooks with the aid of bus transport, although arguably he would have a harder job today. Even if you have access to a car, there is something invigorating about leaving it at home for the day and doing a walk via public transport – you will feel very smug afterwards. However, please bear in mind that in the brave new world of deregulation bus routes can come and go with alarming swiftness. For up-to-date information, it is always worth contacting the local operators or popping into the nearest tourist information centre.

The main bus operator for Cumbria is:
> Stagecoach Cumberland
> PO Box 17
> Tangier Street
> Whitehaven
> Cumbria CA28 7XF
> Telephone 01946 63222

There is also a TravelLink information service operated by Cumbria County Council. It offers boat, train and bus times for the Lake District and is available by telephone Monday to Friday and Saturday morning (office hours only). Tel: 01228 812812. Alternatively, write to:
> TravelLink
> Cumbria County Council
> Citadel Chambers
> Carlisle CA3 8SG

Ask for their *To & Through The Lakes*, a free leaflet which has a handy map of bus and boat routes in Cumbria.

One welcome development in recent years has been the involvement of the National Trust, which runs a bus service in Borrowdale during the summer.

For train services, ring 0345 484950.

For lake launches, see the Visitor Attractions listed in Walks 6, 16, 22 and 24.

APPENDIX 3
USEFUL ADDRESSES AND FURTHER INFORMATION

In this section you will find general information about the Lake District, including addresses and/or telephone numbers for tourist information centres, National Park organizations and, most important, the Lake District Weatherline.

LAKE DISTRICT NATIONAL PARK

The Lake District is the largest of the 12 national parks in England and Wales, covering an area of 2265sq km (885sq miles). It was created in 1951 and is administered by the Lake District National Park Authority (NPA), a statutory body which receives most of its funding from government and local councils. Very little of the land within the park is owned by the NPA; unlike national parks in the United States and other European countries, the countryside within the park boundary is privately owned.

The statutory aims of the NPA are to conserve the natural beauty, wildlife and cultural heritage of the Lake District, to promote opportunities for enjoyment and understanding of the national park, and to foster the interests of the local community. The NPA operates as one of the planning authorities for the area and is also heavily involved in maintenance, countryside access and promotion of the area through its information and visitor centres. It also produces a range of publications about the area, which you can find in any of its information centres (see page 155).

You are most likely to encounter the NPA through its information centres or by bumping into one of its rangers. These individuals patrol the park, working on footpath maintenance, liaising with farmers over access, offering advice and policing the by-laws. They are supported by around 350 voluntary wardens, who give their time to work with the NPA.

The Lake District NPA runs public events and activities throughout the year, from working days with a ranger to children's picnics at Brockhole. These are all listed in the *Events* booklet, available from information centres.

To contact the administrative headquarters of the National Park Authority, write to:
Lake District National Park Authority
Murley Moss
Oxenholme Road
Kendal
Cumbria LA9 7RL

NATIONAL PARK VISITOR CENTRE

The NPA runs the National Park Visitor Centre at Brockhole, Windermere. This is an ex-mansion house on the shore of Windermere with extensive grounds and lovely gardens. You can catch a boat to Brockhole from Waterhead or Bowness and picnic in the grounds, making it a good waterside potter in its own right. Brockhole is home to a range of events throughout the season and is also a good source of general information about the Lakes. It is open daily, April to November, admission free (although there is a parking charge).

> National Park Visitor Centre
> Brockhole
> Windermere
> Cumbria LA23 1LJ
> Tel: 015394 46601

THE NATIONAL TRUST

The National Trust should not to be confused with the National Park Authority. Both were formed to care for and conserve the countryside and promote enjoyment of the area, and both run information centres and have rangers (although the National Trust calls them wardens). However, the National Trust is a registered charity, receiving its money from donations and from income generated from its properties. Also, unlike the NPA, it owns all the land it cares for, which, in the case of the Lake District, is around a quarter of the area within the national park boundary.

The National Trust for Places of Historic Interest or Natural Beauty – to give it its full title – has strong historic links with the Lake District. The ideas which formed the basis for the movement were propounded by the writer and philosopher John Ruskin in the late nineteenth century. Indeed, it was the climate of opinion generated by opposition to the Thirlmere reservoir (see Walk 19: Thirlmere & Harrop Tarn) which fostered the birth of the Trust. The Trust was officially registered on 12 January 1895 and one of its three founder members was Canon Hardwicke Rawnsley, vicar of Crosthwaite and Canon of Carlisle. The Trust's first property was Brandlehow Woods, acquired in 1902 (see Walk 24: Derwent Water).

The Trust owns a number of famous houses in the Lake District, including Townend, a wonderful statesman farmer's house in Troutbeck, near Windermere, and Hill Top, Beatrix Potter's home at Near Sawrey. For a full list of properties and information centres in the Lake District, contact:

> The National Trust
> North West Regional Office
> The Hollens
> Grasmere
> Cumbria LA22 9QZ
> Tel: 015394 35599

TOURIST INFORMATION CENTRES

There are tourist information centres (TICs) in all towns and most major villages in Cumbria. They vary from small corner shops which give out local information to large, networked TICs which can book you into accommodation on the other side of the country. The centres run by the Lake District NPA are particularly useful for walking advice and information, and often have excellent exhibitions and a range of publications specifically about the national park.

LAKE DISTRICT NATIONAL PARK INFORMATION CENTRES

	Telephone	*Opening*
Bowness-on-Windermere	015394 42895	Closed winter
Broughton-in-Furness	01229 716115	
Coniston	015394 41533	Closed winter
Glenridding	017684 82414	Closed winter
Grasmere	015394 35245	Closed winter
Hawkshead	015394 36525	Closed winter
Keswick Discovery Centre	017687 72803	Closed winter
Pooley Bridge	017684 86530	Closed winter
Seatoller	017687 77294	Closed winter
Waterhead, Ambleside	015394 32729	Closed winter

Broughton-in-Furness is run jointly by the NPA and South Lakeland District Council and is open all year.

Not all the centres are networked, which means they will not offer accommodation booking beyond their immediate area.

In addition, there are 12 Local Information Points (LIPs) where national park information is available in local shops and post offices, mostly in the outlying areas of the Lake District. These can be a good source of information about the immediate locality, but they are not geared up to answer telephone queries.

Barn Door Shop, Wasdale Head
Boot Post Office, Boot, Eskdale
Bampton Post Office, Bampton Grange, Shap
Ennerdale Bridge Post Office, Ennerdale, Nr Cleator Moor
Far Sawrey Post Office, Nr Hawkshead
Forest Spinners, Rusland, Haverthwaite
Gosforth Pottery, Gosforth, Nr Seascale
High Lorton Post Office, Lorton Vale, Nr Cockermouth
Maple Tree Corner Shop, Elterwater
Ravenglass Station Booking Office, Ravenglass & Eskdale Railway, Ravenglass
St Bees Post Office, 122 Main Street, St Bees
Ulpha Post Office, Duddon Valley, Nr Broughton-in-Furness

OTHER TOURIST INFORMATION CENTRES IN CUMBRIA

Unless stated otherwise, these are all open throughout the year. As part of the networked service, they offer accommodation booking and many also operate a bureau de change.

	Telephone	
Alston	01434 381696	
Ambleside	015394 32582	
Appleby	017683 51177	
Barrow-in-Furness	01229 870156	
Brampton	016977 3433	Closed winter
Carlisle	01228 512444	
Cockermouth	01900 822634	
Egremont	01946 820693	
Grange-over-Sands	015395 34026	Closed winter
Kendal	01539 725758	
Keswick	017687 72645	
Killington Lake	015396 20138	
Kirkby Lonsdale	015242 71437	
Kirkby Stephen	017683 71199	
Longtown	01228 791876	
Maryport	01900 813738	
Millom	01229 772555	
Penrith	01768 67466	
Ravenglass	01229 717278	Closed winter
Sedbergh	015396 20125	Closed winter
Silloth-on-Solway	016973 31944	Closed winter
Southwaite	016974 73445/6	
Ulverston	01229 587120	
Whitehaven	01946 695678	
Windermere	015394 46499	
Workington	01900 602923	

The TICs are run by a variety of local authorities, many of which publish their own accommodation guides to the area. These list registered guest houses, hotels, campsites and caravan sites, with contact details and lists of facilities. Contact the nearest TIC to the part of the Lakes you are planning to visit.

CUMBRIA TOURIST BOARD

This is another source of information and accommodation details, particularly on Cumbria as a whole. You will find it useful to contact them prior to your visit.

Cumbria Tourist Board
Ashleigh
Holly Road, Windermere
Cumbria LA23 2AQ
Tel: 015394 44444

TALKING PAGES

A national freephone number for local information centres and attractions.
Tel: 0800 600 900

OTHER ORGANIZATIONS

There are a number of other organizations which work to conserve and protect the Lake District. These are for the committed Lakeland enthusiast. If you care about the area or are feeling guilty about the amount of Lake District soil you scrape off your boots when you get home, you may wish to get involved.

BRITISH TRUST FOR CONSERVATION VOLUNTEERS

The BTCV is Britain's largest practical conservation charity, with over 85,000 volunteers. Anyone can join and help work in a wide range of conservation activities, from building a drystone wall and footpath maintenance to forestry and studying wildlife. The BTCV runs day, weekend and week-long conservation holidays called 'Natural Breaks' and volunteers come from all sections of the community. It is probably the most practical way you can get involved in caring for the Lake District. For more details of this work or a copy of the *Natural Breaks* brochure, contact the BTCV Cumbria office.

British Trust for Conservation Volunteers
National Park Centre
Brockhole
Windermere
Cumbria LA23 1LJ
Tel: 015394 43098

Alternatively, contact the national office.

BTCV Head Office
36 St Mary's Street
Wallingford
Oxfordshire OX10 0EU
Tel: 01491 839766

FRIENDS OF THE LAKE DISTRICT

This is a very worthwhile association which operates as a pressure group to promote and organize concerted action for the protection and conservation of the Lake District. It is very influential and has run a number of extremely successful campaigns in the past. It also represents the Council for the Protection of Rural England (CPRE) and you don't have to live in the area to become a member.

Friends of the Lake District
Number 3
Yard 77
Highgate
Kendal
Cumbria LA9 4ED
Tel: 01539 720788

MOUNTAIN RESCUE PROCEDURE

In the event of serious trouble on the fells, you may need to call out the mountain rescue service. There are a number of teams operating in Cumbria. If a member of your group is hurt, at least one person should stay with the injured party while one or (preferably) two others make their way to the nearest telephone. Dial 999 and ask for the police. They will then call out the appropriate team. If you can, have an accurate OS grid reference to give for the location of the injured person.

Do not call up the mountain rescue on your mobile phone if you are just a bit lost or feeling tired. Members of the mountain rescue teams are volunteers and a call-out will often mean leaving their jobs for many hours. It is a service for emergencies.

LAKE DISTRICT WEATHERLINE

The NPA operates a weather forecasting service, supplied direct by the Newcastle Met Office, which is always more accurate than the national forecasts. It is available 24 hours a day and is updated twice daily. In winter, the forecast includes fell-top conditions supplied by the national park rangers.

Weatherline tel: 017687 75757

INDEX